Proofreading & Editing

Grade 4

Published by Instructional Fair
an imprint of

 **Children's Publishing**

D1515547

Authors: Kelly Hatfield, Rob Hatfield
Project Director/Editor: Kathryn Wheeler
Editor: Diana Wallis

Children's Publishing

Published by Instructional Fair
An imprint of McGraw-Hill Children's Publishing
Copyright © 2004 McGraw-Hill Children's Publishing

Send all inquiries to:
McGraw-Hill Children's Publishing
3195 Wilson Drive NW
Grand Rapids, Michigan 49544

Proofreading & Editing—grade 4
ISBN: 0-7424-2754-4

1 2 3 4 5 6 7 8 9 MAL 09 08 07 06 05 04

Table of Contents

Mark It Right

Authors and editors use special marks to proofread and edit. These are called **proofreading marks.** These marks show how to fix mistakes. When you edit and proofread, you can use these marks, too. They are fast and easy to use.

1. Here is the mark to make a **capital letter:** a̲.

   Example: I live in p̲ortland, Oregon.

Mark this sentence to fix the letters that should be capitals.

   for our vacation, mom is taking us to england!

2. Here is the mark to change a capital letter into a **lowercase letter:** A̸.

   Example: We are G̸oing to London.

Mark this sentence to fix the letters that should be lowercase.

   I want to see the Clock called Big Ben.

3. Here is the mark to **delete,** or take out, a word: ~~and~~.

   Example: We are going to stay with Aunt Anna and ~~and~~ Uncle Peter.

Mark this sentence to take out the extra word.

   After we see London, we are will going to Cambridge.

4. To fix letters that are in the **wrong order,** use this mark: ei.

   Example: We are going to stay with Aunt Anna and Uncle Peter.

Mark this sentence to fix the misspelled word.

   Mom says that travle helps people learn.

4   0-7424-2754-4 *Proofreading & Editing*

Name _____   Date _____

Mark It Right (cont.)

5. Here is the mark to put something **into** a sentence: ∧.
   When you add a comma, put it **inside** the mark. ⩕

   Mom would like to travel to Ireland∧England∧and France someday.

   When you **add** a word, a period, a question mark, a quotation mark, or an exclamation mark, use the mark to show the place. Then write the word or punctuation mark **above** the place.

   Mom would like to travel to ∧ someday.
   (Ireland)

Put the missing punctuation and words into this sentence.

   Look   There's the Tower London!

6. Here is the mark to show the start of a **new paragraph:** ¶.

   Example: ¶ Today, we are flying home again.

Use the paragraph mark to show where the new paragraph starts.

   Last year, my summer vacation was lots of fun. My

   grandparents took me to see Niagara Falls and Montreal.

   This summer, Mom and I are flying to London. We will see

   many sights in the city. We will also visit a town in the

   countryside.

Now use the proofreading marks you have learned to edit these sentences.

7. mom and I Will eat a special dish called Fish and chips

8. At the end of the trip we will stop to see my Grandparents before coming home

At the End

When you are editing punctuation, remember:

A **statement** ends with a period (.).

　　We are studying about the Underground Railroad**.**

A **question** ends with a question mark (?).

　　Do you know about it**?**

An **exclamation** ends with an exclamation point (!).

　　Those people were brave**!**

A **command** can end with a period or an exclamation point.

　　Watch out**!**

　　Find the next safe house**.**

This is the mark to add punctuation:　⌄.

Mark the sentences to add the missing punctuation.

1. Tiana had an ancestor who escaped from the South

2. Did you learn about Harriet Tubman

3. I want to visit an Underground Railroad station

4. What　　There is one in our town

5. That's exciting news

Melissa wrote a report about her class field trip. Proofread her report. Use this mark ⌄ to put in missing punctuation. Use this mark ⟩ to take out punctuation that is wrong.

6. 　　　On Friday! our class went on a field trip We were so excited

　　　We went to see an old house in our town It used to be a hiding place for people It

　　was a station on the Underground Railroad "Is there a secret room here " we asked.

　　There was It was behind a wall in the cellar The door had shelves on the outside When

　　it was closed, it looked just like part of the wall

7. Write your own sentence about a field trip. Be sure to use correct punctuation.

　　_____

　　_____

　　　　6　　　　0-7424-2754-4 *Proofreading & Editing*

Name _____ Date _____

Journal Journeys

Editors need to make sure that each sentence ends with the right punctuation.

A **statement** ends with a **period** (.).

I keep a journal**.**

A **question** ends with a **question mark** (?).

Do you like to write**?**

An **exclamation** ends with an **exclamation point** (!).

My journal is missing**!**

A **command** can end with a **period** or an **exclamation point.**

Help me look for my journal**.** Hurry**!**

Add the correct punctuation in the blanks at the end of each sentence. This is the mark to add punctuation: ∧**.**

(1) What do you think students should write about _____ (2) If you said, "Things that they know," you are right _____ It is easy to write about things we know _____ (3) Hobbies, family, friends, and school events can provide us with many ideas _____ (4) That is why in many classrooms, students write in journals every day _____ (5) If you do not keep a journal in school, you could begin keeping one at home _____ (6) Think of what fun it would be to read it 20 years from now _____ (7) Do you think you would remember the boy in your fourth-grade class who could talk like Donald Duck _____ (8) Would you remember how proud you were of the A on your math test _____ (9) A journal will help your writing. It will also bring back good memories years later _____

Use proofreading marks to add punctuation to the ends of these sentences.

10. When will you write in your journal _____

11. I have my journal from third grade _____

12. Write faster _____

13. Can I read what you wrote _____

7 0-7424-2754-4 *Proofreading & Editing*

More Journal Journeys

Editors must check the punctuation inside sentences. Here are some ways that commas are used in sentences and phrases:

in **dates:**   November 4, 2004

in **addresses:**   Columbus, Ohio

in **a series:**   pens, pencils, and paper

in **prepositional phrases:**   Before I kept a journal, I had a scrapbook.

in **compound sentences before the conjunction:**
   I put my journal on my desk, and it was gone five minutes later.

Use this mark to add a comma: ⋏ .

Use this mark to delete, or take out, a comma: ℓ .

Add or delete commas in these sentences.

1. Along with helping you remember things journals help you learn to write better.

2. For example say you wanted to write about a funny experience, you had at school

3. You can look it up, in your journal, and you can read about it.

4. My journal is about my life in Denver Colorado.

5. I have my second-grade journals and I have a journal from third grade.

6. Journals make writing, fun!

Use proofreading marks to fix the punctuation in these sentences.

7. It was my brother, who took my journal

8. My teacher gave me a new blank book and I used it to start a journal

9. Did you see, the new book about keeping a journal?

Exploring Punctuation

When you are proofreading punctuation, remember:

A **comma** goes **after a prepositional phrase.**

In the 1600s, there were many explorers.

A **comma** goes **between the names of a city and a country.**

La Salle's birthplace was Rouen, France.

Commas go **between words in a series.**

Henry Hudson explored the Hudson River, Delaware Bay, and Chesapeake Bay.

An **apostrophe** shows a **contraction.**

We're going to study explorers this month.

A **period** goes **after an abbreviation.**

Ms. Rodriguez told us all about La Salle.

Hudson went to the place where Albany, N.Y., is today.

Periods go **after initials.**

Someday, I may be famous: Elisa M. Watson, explorer!

This is the mark to add punctuation: You're.

Circle the choice that shows the missing punctuation mark.

1. Ms. Rodriguez showed us a picture of Henry Hudson.
   a. .
   b. ,
   c. !
   d. None

2. In the spring of 1611 Hudson disappeared.
   a. .
   b. ,
   c. !
   d. None

3. We re going to draw a map of explorers' routes.
   a. '
   b. .
   c. "
   d. None

4. I want to see Baltimore Maryland, on the Chesapeake Bay.
   a. !
   b. ,
   c. "
   d. None

Mark the sentences for missing punctuation.

5. Along with his son Hudson was set adrift in a boat

6. We ll never know what happened to them.

7. You can drive to Hudson Bay, through Ontario Canada.

Columbus

Quotation marks show someone's exact words. When you proofread quotation marks, remember:

Put quotation marks **outside** of the punctuation that is part of the quote.

Capitalize the first word of the quote, unless the quote is the second part of a sentence.

Use a comma, a question mark, or an exclamation point to divide a quotation from the rest of the sentence.

"How long until Columbus Day?" asked Maya.

Ms. Rodriguez replied, "Only five more days! Are you looking forward to our class party?"

This is the mark to add punctuation: "Hi!"

Place quotation marks in these sentences.

1. I think Columbus was very brave, said Jonathan.

2. When he set sail, he didn't know if he would ever reach land again, Tiana said. I bet his crew was scared.

3. Their journey must have been hard, Ms. Rodriguez added. But the crew must have trusted Columbus.

4. I would have wanted to go home! said Yong.

5. If they had gone home, said Maria, then we wouldn't be here today!

6. Good point, Maria! said Ms. Rodriguez.

7. What will we do, asked Tiana, at our party?

8. Ms. Rodriguez said, We are going to play a game about explorers.

Name _____ Date _____

A Letter From Steven

Letters have special punctuation. When you are editing a letter, remember:

There is a comma **between the date and the year.**

There is a comma **after the greeting.**

There is a comma **after the closing.**

This is the mark to add punctuation: ⋏ .

This is the mark to take out punctuation that is wrong: ℐ .

We went to the store on April⟋22, 2004.

Use the marks you have learned to fix the punctuation in this letter.

June 30 2004

Dear Mom

Grandma Grandpa and I are having a great time here at the cabin. I thought I would be bored but there is so much to do We go out in the canoe Yesterday, Grandma and I paddled to the store in Two Rivers We saw deer on the shore as we went by Grandpa and I stacked firewood together We play games every evening. I am getting great at *Go Fish*

Late last night Grandpa and I went out on the deck Guess what we saw A whole family of raccoons The mother had two babies with her The babies were so cute The mother kept watching me Hold very still, said Grandpa Finally, they took their food and went down to the lake I will never forget watching them

Are you having fun with your painting How is Becca doing in her dance class Please write soon and tell me all about the big birthday party Say hi to everybody for me.

Love

Steven

One Summer Morning

Use this mark to add punctuation: ⌃ Can we go now? ⌃

Use this mark to take out incorrect punctuation: ℐ.

I want to write about a pioneer girl?ℐ

1. Use proofreading marks to correct the punctuation in this story.

Carrie looked across the prairie from her doorstep! The prairie looked like the sea The grass moved in the wind just like waves But there was not a single tree in sight How I miss the shade thought Carrie and how I miss our old home! She wiped her forehead on her sleeve It was early in the morning but already it was hot In her long skirts and sunbonnet Carrie felt as though she was being roasted over a fire

Carrie! called Mama from the fireplace Please come in here and help me with breakfast

Carrie sighed Cooking over the open fire was so hot but there had been no room in the wagon for a stove Carrie had been lucky that she got to take a few small things in her trunk: her diary her doll and a china box

Carrie looked out at the fields where Papa was hard at work Then she turned to go back into the sod house and start the chores of the day

2. Write another sentence for this story. Be sure to use correct punctuation.

_____

_____

Inspiring Leaders

Names are always capitalized. These include people's first and last names, the names of groups or tribes, and the names of pets.

    Wilma **M**ankiller belongs to the **C**herokee tribe.

People's titles are capitalized when they go in front of their names.

    Chief Mankiller is an important person.

If the title follows the name, it is not capitalized.

    Wilma Mankiller was the **c**hief of her tribe.

This is the mark to capitalize a letter: joseph.

This is the mark to turn a capital letter into a lowercase letter: King.

Circle the choice that shows correct capitalization.

1.   a.   miguel learned about
       b.   the Culture
       c.   of the Cherokee.

2.   a.   The Iroquois
       b.   were Native americans who
       c.   lived in the Forest.

3.   a.   alyson Rider
       b.   likes to Read about
       c.   the Cheyenne people.

Mark the sentences to correct the capitalization.

4.   red cloud helped win land for the Lakota tribe.

5.   chief Joseph was a famous nineteenth-century leader.

6.   Today, Wilma mankiller lives in Oklahoma.

7.   Mankiller is still an important leader of the cherokee people.

Native-American Places

Names of places are capitalized.

    The state of Ohio has many Native-American burial mounds.

    One burial mound is near the town of Aberdeen.

This is the mark to capitalize a letter: o̲hio.

This is the mark to turn a capital letter into a lowercase letter: S̸tate.

Circle the choice that shows correct capitalization.

1.   a.   We live In
     b.   St. Ignace, Michigan,
     c.   near the Museum of ojibwa Culture.

2.   a.   The city of cheyenne
     b.   was named for the Tribe
     c.   who lived in Wyoming.

3.   a.   Mystic, Connecticut,
     b.   is the Town where
     c.   the pequot tribe once had a fort.

4.   Use proofreading marks to fix the capitalization in this story.

    Long before Europeans came to america, many different tribes settled the land. One famous tribe was the Iroquois. The Iroquois lived in the mountains of new york and pennsylvania. The Ojibwa lived in michigan and in other places around the Great Lakes. The Lakota tribe was strong and powerful. They lived on the prairie in north Dakota and south dakota. In idaho, the Nez Percé was a peaceful tribe of traders and horse trainers.

Janna's Schedule

The names of the days and months are always capitalized.

This is the mark to capitalize a letter: <u>m</u>onday.

This is the mark to turn a capital letter into a lowercase letter: Ⱦay.

Circle the choice that shows the right capitalization.

1. a.   Janna's recital is Tuesday, october 24.
     b.   Janna's recital is tuesday, october 24.
     c.   Janna's recital is Tuesday, October 24.

2. a.   Janna has ballet on mondays and Wednesdays.
     b.   Janna has ballet on Mondays and Wednesdays.
     c.   Janna has ballet on mondays and wednesdays.

3. a.   Janna dances from september to May.
     b.   Janna dances from September to May.
     c.   Janna dances from september to may.

Mark the sentences to fix the capitalization.

4.   Do you think Janna can Sleep over on Friday or saturday?

5.   Janna is going to a concert on friday, April 4.

6.   friday's concert tickets are for janna's birthday.

7.   janna goes to Swimming lessons during july and August.

8.   Her favorite day of the week is monday.

9.   janna is moving to a new house next saturday.

10. She will start school on wednesday, september 4.

     15   0-7424-2754-4 *Proofreading & Editing*

All About Bears

Remember, use this mark to capitalize the first letter of a sentence: the.

Use this mark to turn a capital letter into a lowercase letter: Bear.

Capitalize the first word in a sentence and the names of people, places, months, and titles.

Use proofreading marks to fix the capitalization in each sentence.

1. a bear can eat 35 pounds of fish at a time.

2. some bears weigh almost 2,000 pounds.

3. the stuffed teddy bear was named after president theodore roosevelt.

4. most bear cubs are born in november.

5. bears are found in many states.

6. the north American grizzly bear is rare in the United states.

7. There is a famous short story called "the bear."

8. In asia, bears are trained to dance.

9. panda bears from china are not really bears.

10. Brown bears are found in asia, europe, and north america.

Write two sentences about bears. Be sure to use correct capitalization.

11. _____

_____

_____

_____

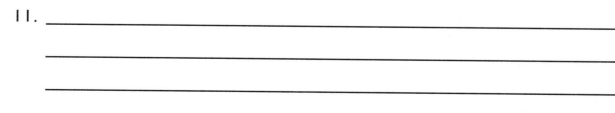

Name _____   Date _____

An American Hero

Use this mark to capitalize a letter: <u>a</u>frican American.

Use this mark to make a capital letter into a lowercase letter: ⱢBus.

1.   Use proofreading marks to fix the capitalization in this story.

Rosa parks was a brave African-american woman who helped make our Country a better place. Until 1955, african-american people in montgomery, Alabama, had to give up their bus seats to white People. When a white person wanted a Seat, the African-American person had to move to the back of the bus or stand in the Aisle. But Rosa parks believed that this city law was wrong. One day she said she would not give up her Seat. Because of this, Rosa was arrested.

Many americans were very angry that Rosa was arrested. She had stood up—rather, she had sat down—for what was fair and Right. People stopped using the Buses, causing the City to lose money. Finally, the United states Supreme court said that the city's bus law was wrong. Because of Rosa parks's bravery, a wrong was turned into a Right.

Circle the correct capitalization of each phrase.

2.   a.   Montgomery, Alabama
     b.   montgomery, Alabama
     c.   montgomery, alabama

3.   a.   equal rights
     b.   Equal rights
     c.   equal Rights

4.   a.   Supreme court
     b.   supreme court
     c.   Supreme Court

5.   a.   city law
     b.   City law
     c.   city Law

Name _____   Date _____

Fashion Sense

When you proofread, look for spelling mistakes. You can use proofreading marks to fix these.

If there is just one extra letter, use this mark to take it out: frie̶end.

If the word is spelled wrong, use the same mark to take out the whole word. Then write the word with the right spelling above the place.   *mineral* ̶m̶i̶n̶a̶r̶e̶l̶

To fix letters that are in the wrong order, use this mark: frei͡nd.

Circle the choice that shows the right spelling of the word.

1. This _____ is for gym.
    a. uniforme
    b. unifurm
    c. uniform
    d. unieform

2. That dress costs three _____ dollars!
    a. hundred
    b. hunedred
    c. hunderd
    d. hundread

3. Did you finish the _____ yet?
    a. blouze
    b. blous
    c. blousse
    d. blouse

4. My new shirt has _____ on it.
    a. daisyes
    b. daisies
    c. daisys
    d. daises

5. He _____ stained his jacket.
    a. acidentaly
    b. accidentally
    c. acdentaly
    d. acidentally

Use proofreading marks to fix the spelling in these sentences.

6. Everyone loves to waer blue jeens.

7. I have a new pair of runing shoes.

Name _____ Date _____

Sounds the Same!

Homophones are pairs of words that sound like each other but are spelled differently and have different meanings.

    red read

When you proofread, watch for homophones.
Sometimes the wrong word is written. Use this mark to change it: ℓ.

    The toy car was ~~read~~. *red*

Read the clues and write the homophones.

1. The homophone for <u>hoarse</u>: _____

2. The time word that is a homophone for <u>weak</u>: _____

3. Two homophones for <u>two</u>: _____

4. An animal name that is a homophone for <u>hair</u>: _____

5. A homophone for <u>plain</u>: _____

6. A habitat homophone for <u>see</u>: _____

Use proofreading marks to fix the homophones in these sentences.

7. That jacket was cheep.

8. I am two tired to go to the movies.

9. Did you by a pear of pants?

10. It was a dark and stormy knight.

          0-7424-2754-4 *Proofreading & Editing*

Name _____ Date _____

Another Word?

Sometimes editors must change one word to another. Sometimes an editor does this to make a sentence simpler or easier to read or to make the sentence sound better. Editors need to choose **synonyms,** words that mean about the same thing.

Read each phrase. Choose the word that means the same or about the same as the underlined word.

1. fast <u>vehicle</u>
   a. runner
   b. animal
   c. car
   d. computer

2. To be <u>healthy</u> is to be—
   a. slow
   b. well
   c. active
   d. ill

3. attend a <u>conference</u>
   a. party
   b. game
   c. meeting
   d. race

4. <u>beautiful</u> painting
   a. pretty
   b. interesting
   c. colorful
   d. light

5. <u>repair</u> the car
   a. clean
   b. drive
   c. fix
   d. sell

Replace the underlined word in the sentence with a synonym. Write your word choice on the line.

6. We found the lemonade <u>refreshing</u>. _____

7. How <u>lengthy</u> is the test? _____

8. We took a <u>leisurely</u> walk. _____

20 0-7424-2754-4 *Proofreading & Editing*

Velvet's Class

Editors make lots of choices when they work on a piece of writing. They must make sure that the correct words are used. If they see words that aren't correct in the sentence, they change them.

Angella wrote a story about her dog, Velvet. She made some mistakes with word choices. Read each sentence. Then circle the correct word to replace the underlined word or words.

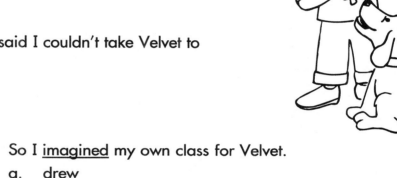

1. My dog Velvet knows lots of tricks and is very <u>cleaver</u>.
    a. clean
    b. clever
    c. clinging

2. I was <u>dismal</u> when Mom said I couldn't take Velvet to training classes.
    a. disappointed
    b. happy
    c. diseased

3. So I <u>imagined</u> my own class for Velvet.
    a. drew
    b. created
    c. dreamed

4. I could not believe how <u>rabidly</u> Velvet learned her lessons!
    a. rapidly
    b. angrily
    c. selfishly

5. All of Velvet 's bad habits <u>vented</u> after our classes.
    a. vanished
    b. vanity
    c. vandal

6. Write another sentence about Velvet and Angella. Make sure you use words that say what you mean.

    _____

    _____

Name _____ Date _____

Don't Do It!

Editors must look at lots of things in a piece of writing. One thing they check for is **double negatives.**

I <u>don't</u> have <u>no</u> books.

If you see a double negative, use this mark to take it out: ⌐___ℓ.
Then write the correct word or words above the place.

Circle the best phrase to replace the underlined phrase.

1. Everybody knows <u>I didn't mean nothing</u> by it.
   a. did mean nothing
   b. didn't mean none
   c. didn't mean anything

2. You <u>haven't seen nothing</u> yet.
   a. have seen nothing
   b. haven't seen none
   c. haven't seen anything

3. This <u>isn't any good neither</u>.
   a. isn't none good neither
   b. isn't any good either
   c. isn't nothing good neither

4. He <u>wouldn't do no work</u>.
   a. wouldn't do any work
   b. would not do no work
   c. would do any work

5. I <u>couldn't find it nowhere</u>.
   a. could find it nowhere
   b. couldn't find it nohow
   c. couldn't find it anywhere

Use proofreading marks to fix the double negatives in these sentences.

6. I didn't have no money.

7. I can't hardly wait to go.

8. I didn't know nobody there.

   0-7424-2754-4 *Proofreading & Editing*

Many Meanings

Editors must make lots of choices when they work on a piece of writing. They must make sure that the correct words are used. Some words have more than one meaning, so an editor makes sure that those words are used the way the writer meant them to be used.

Choose the answer in which the word is used the same way as in the sentence.

1. Please <u>file</u> these papers.

    a. The counselor pulled out her <u>file</u> on the Jones family.
    b. Sally used a <u>file</u> to smooth her fingernails.
    c. I put the <u>file</u> cards in order.
    d. Jane asked her secretary to <u>file</u> the reports on water safety.

2. I used a <u>lemon</u> to make lemonade.

    a. The color of the baby's room is <u>lemon</u>.
    b. That car was a <u>lemon</u>.
    c. This cleaner has a lovely <u>lemon</u> scent.
    d. Rachel bought a <u>lemon</u> at the store.

3. She could not reach the right <u>note</u> on the piano.

    a. Please make a <u>note</u> of this change.
    b. I wrote a <u>note</u> so you will not forget.
    c. The musical <u>note</u> he asked us to play was C.
    d. <u>Note</u> the large size of the buildings.

Circle the word that works in both sentences.

4. The player began to _____ .
    Put the new _____ on the car.

    a. run
    b. fender
    c. weaken
    d. tire

5. Do you feel _____ ?
    We get our water from a _____ .

    a. well
    b. good
    c. pipe
    d. sick

6. Mrs. Johnson said Carrie was a _____ student.
    The light from the headlights was _____ .

    a. noisy
    b. red
    c. bright
    d. hardworking

7. The surface of the car was _____ .
    Mr. Abed gave a _____ speech.

    a. red
    b. dirty
    c. painted
    d. dull

Many Monsters

Editors make sure the verbs in a sentence agree with the number of the subjects in the sentence. When verbs are regular, present-tense verbs, you can check them like this:

If the subject is **one** noun or pronoun (he, she, it), add an **s** to the verb.

   The **monster** eat**s** the car.

If the subject is **I, you,** or **more than one** person, place, or thing, do not add an *s* to the verb.

   I see a monster!   **Monsters live** in caves.

For the irregular verb *to be,* use **is** for one noun or pronoun. Use **are** for more than one subject. Use **am** for *I*.

   We are happy at the movies.   **I am** happy at the movies.
   She is happy at the movies.

Read each sentence aloud. Circle the form of the verb that matches the subject.

1. People (like, likes) to see movies about monsters.

2. Some monsters (look, looks) very scary on the screen.

3. King Kong (look, looks) huge!

4. But he (is, are) really just a small rubber model.

5. Today, artists (use, uses) computers to make many movie monsters.

6. They (is, are) able to create many different effects with the computer.

7. Monsters (is, are) scarier than ever now!

Use proofreading marks to fix the mistakes in these sentences.

8. My sister love to go to the movies.

9. We sits up in the balcony.

10. My mom buy us popcorn.

Many Monsters (cont.)

When a piece of writing is written in past tense, the subject and verb still must agree. Most past-tense verbs have *–ed* on the end of the verb. But there are also **irregular** verbs that do not follow the *–ed* rule. The verb **to be** is one irregular verb. Other examples are **to come, to make, to give,** and **to say.**

Read each choice aloud. Circle the one in which the subject and verb agree.

11.   a. Yesterday, the frogs was at the edge of the river.
       b. They came to find some spiders to eat.
       c. Frogs scares me.

12.   a. One green frog hopped out of the water.
       b. He were very shiny.
       c. He look for a bug.

13.   a. I think frogs looks like little monsters.
       b. They is green with big, black eyes.
       c. A frog is not my favorite animal!

Use proofreading marks to edit the verbs in the following sentences.
Use this mark to take out letters or words that don't belong: 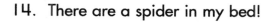 .
Use this mark to add letters: ∧ .

14.   There are a spider in my bed!

15.   I screams when I see it.

16.   My mom run into the room.

17.   I see the spider as it run across the room.

18.   Mom pick it up on a newspaper and takes it outside.

19.   I make my bed again and tucks in the sheets tightly.

20.   If another spider show up, it won't be able to get in!

Awful Ellen

Editors must remember to look for grammar mistakes as they proofread. When you read a story, use proofreading marks to fix the mistakes you find.

Use this mark to add a word or phrase: ∧.

If there is just one extra letter in a misspelled word, use this mark: letteer.

If a whole word is wrong, use the same mark to take out the whole word. Then write another word above the place.   inform form

Remember to check that words are used correctly in sentences. Make sure that verbs agree with the number of subjects and that verbs are the right tense.

Use proofreading marks to fix the mistakes in these sentences.

1. My cousin Ellen are just awful!

2. Whenever she comes to our house, someone get into trouble.

3. She always talk us into doing something we're not supposed to do.

4. She won't let anybody say nothing about it, either.

5. One time, Ellen tolds everybody to skip balls against Mrs. White's house.

6. My brother threws the ball against a window.

7. Nobody else did nothing while we listened to the breaking glass.

8. Mrs. White stroll out of the house.

9. Everybody say, "It was Ellen's idea!"

10. Mrs. White didn't care what nobody said, though.

Awful Ellen (cont.)

Circle the kind of mistake in each sentence.

11. We didn't listen to nobody.

    a. wrong word
    b. double negative
    c. subject-verb agreement problem

12. We is Ellen's cousins.

    a. wrong word
    b. double negative
    c. subject-verb agreement problem

13. Ellen was well some of the time.

    a. wrong word
    b. double negative
    c. subject-verb agreement problem

14. Look for grammar mistakes in the story. Use proofreading marks to fix them.

> One summer, my cousin Ellen camed to stay with us. It was the bad summer of my life! It seemed as though we was in trouble every single day. One day, Ellen says that we was all going fishing. We borrowed somebody's boat . . . and we didn't ask, neither.
>
> Another day, Ellen thought it were a fun idea to run away and join the circus. She was going to be the circus star. The rest of us would have jobs cleaning up and selling tickets. Even though we weren't not going to get the cool jobs, we still did what Ellen say.
>
> "Why do you always do what Ellen hints you to do?" my mother asked one day. That was after Ellen took us on a hike. I get poison ivy. I couldn't never explain it to her. Ellen had this power. She mades us think that everything would turn out all right. Sometimes it did—like the day Ellen talked us into picking blueberries. Now that were a good day!

 0-7424-2754-4 *Proofreading & Editing*

◆◆◆◆◆◆◆◆◆◆◆◆◆◆◆◆◆◆◆◆◆◆◆◆◆◆◆◆◆◆◆◆◆◆◆◆◆

Home Alone

Editors make lots of choices when they work on a piece of writing. They must make sure that the correct words are used. If they see a word that isn't correct in the sentence, they change it.

◆◆◆◆◆◆◆◆◆◆◆◆◆◆◆◆◆◆◆◆◆◆◆◆◆◆◆◆◆◆◆◆◆◆◆◆◆

Read the start of Hua's story. For each underlined word or phrase, choose a better word and write it on the lines below.

"Are you sure you're going to be all right at home alone?" Chen's mother asked.

"Yes, Mom," Chen replied, trying not to (1) <u>role</u> her eyes. "I'm old enough to stay here for three hours without you."

Chen's mom and dad were going to a cookout that afternoon. Since kids weren't invited, Chen was staying home alone. It was the first time her parents had left her home by herself, and they were (2) <u>conferred</u>. But Chen was sure she could (3) <u>cope</u> it. She was not (4) <u>wearied</u>.

"Let me give you a last-minute quiz to make sure," her dad said. Chen's father was a teacher, and he was always giving her little tests. "What happens if somebody calls and asks for your mom or me?"

"I tell them that you are busy and can't come to the phone right now," Chen said. "Then I take a (5) <u>mess</u>."

"What if there is a (6) <u>hit</u> on the door?" asked her dad.

"I don't answer it because I can't let anyone in anyway."

"Okay, here's a tough one." Her father looked very serious. "What if you hear ghosts in the closets?"

"Dad!" Chen (7) <u>wept</u>. "Don't be so silly! I'll be fine!"

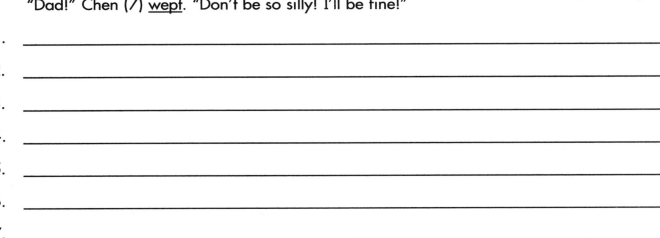

1. _____

2. _____

3. _____

4. _____

5. _____

6. _____

7. _____

Terrific Titles

Editors make lots of choices when they work on a piece of writing. Editors must check the title of a piece of writing. The title should be a good match for the main idea and purpose of the piece. A good title doesn't always repeat the topic. A title should be interesting so the reader will want to read more.

Read the topics for these different pieces of writing. Then circle the best title for each piece.

1. A newspaper article about a big storm
   a. "Learn About Tornadoes"
   b. "Bobby and the Big Storm"
   c. "Big Storm Hits Centerville"

2. A poem about the first snow of winter
   a. "How Snow Is Formed"
   b. "A Blanket of Quiet"
   c. "The Science of Snowflakes"

3. A humorous story about a nature hike during which everything goes wrong
   a. "My Day on the Trail"
   b. "Nature Trails: A Field-Trip Guide"
   c. "Nightmare on the Nature Trail"

4. A class newsletter article about the fourth-grade teachers
   a. "Terrific Teachers: Grade Four"
   b. "How to Teach Fourth Grade"
   c. "About Ms. Rodriguez"

5. A story about a lost cat named Rocket
   a. "Cat Behavior"
   b. "Rocket As a Kitten"
   c. "Rocket 's Quest"

6. A story, written like a diary, about a boy who wants to become a knight
   a. "A Page at Court"
   b. "The History of England"
   c. "Jousting"

Write titles for each piece of writing.

7. An essay about your favorite relative: _____

8. A story about your scariest experience: _____

Big Facts

When you proofread, you need to check punctuation, capitalization, spelling, and grammar. Then use proofreading marks to fix mistakes.

Use this mark to add punctuation or a word: ∧.

Use this mark to capitalize a letter: united States.

Use this mark to make a capital letter into a lowercase letter: ice Cream.

If there is just one extra letter in a word, use this mark: letteer.

To fix letters that are in the wrong order, use this mark: ie.

If a word is wrong or spelled wrong, use the same mark to take out the whole word. Then write the word with the right spelling above the place.   central
sentril

Use proofreading marks to fix these sentences.

1. The largest ice cream sundae weighed over 10,000 pounds

2. high school students and the friendly ice cream company made it in 1980

3. the biggest snowfall were in colorado in april 1921

4. it snowed 76 inches in 24 huors.

5. The largest diamond were found in a mine in south africa

6. it weigh over one and a half pounds

7. Wilma williams came to 265 different schools when she was a child

8. author william faulkner wroted one of the longest sentences in the world

9. There was more than 1300 words! in it.

10. americans, love pizza, and they eat
    75 acres of pizza every day.

11. Americans eat 5,000 tons of candy a dya.

12. americans drink 17 million gallons of coffee and 6 million gallons of tea a day

Mary's Letter

Mary is sending a letter to her aunt and uncle. She wants to thank them for the birthday gift they sent her. She has asked you to look at the letter before she sends it and to mark any mistakes in capitalization, punctuation, spelling, and grammar.

1. Use proofreading marks to fix the mistakes in Mary's letter.

9545 barberry Lane

Richmond, virginia

September 20, 2004

Dear Aunt Margaret and Uncle bob,

     Thank you so much for the sweater! i don't have no red

one like this it fits perfectly I have will wear it with my Blue

jeans

     My Birthday was lots of fun. Did mom tell you about it I gived a party for my

freinds Mom even asked lucy she came all the way from collinswood We plays games

and I gave out prizes My cake was chocelite with pink topping

     i asked my mom about when i can visit you. she said that maybe I can visit during

my christmas vacation. does that sound good to you I'll let you know if we talks any

more about it. i would be so excited! Thank You again for thinking of me when I m so

far away. I hope to see you soon

        your niece

        Mary

2. Write one more sentence to add to Mary's letter. Be sure to use correct grammar and spelling.

_____

_____

Name _____   Date _____

Faraway Places

A **sentence** is a group of words that has a subject and a predicate and tells a complete thought. A **fragment** is not a complete sentence. Editors must fix fragments and make them into sentences. In the following sentences, the subject is underlined once and the predicate is underlined twice.

sentences: Paris is in France.

I went to Tokyo many years ago.

Mexico City is very large.

fragments: Budapest, the capital of Hungary (no predicate)

in the beautiful city of Venice (no subject or predicate)

Because Bombay is so old (not a complete thought)

Write **S** on the line before each sentence. Write **F** on the line before each fragment.

1. _____   Tel Aviv is in Israel.

2. _____   The cities of Sparta and Athens.

3. _____   St. Petersburg used to be called Leningrad.

4. _____   Cape Town is near the Cape of Good Hope.

5. _____   Because no one lives in the city of Machu Picchu.

6. _____   The town of Alice Springs is in the middle of Australia.

Read the following paragraph. Underline the fragments. Then rewrite the fragments to make complete sentences. (Hint: Sometimes you can fix a fragment by making it part of another sentence.)

Pamplona is a city in northern Spain. A very old city. Every year, the city has a festival. Bulls are set loose. They run through the city streets. People come from around the world. They run through the streets with the bulls. Because running with the bulls can be dangerous. People are sometimes hurt.

7. _____

_____

8. _____

_____

Ghost Towns

Editors need to know when different kinds of sentences are correct.

A **simple sentence** has a subject and a predicate and expresses a complete thought. Either the subject or the predicate may be compound.

<u>Aurora and Gold Point</u> <u>are ghost towns in Nevada</u>.
      subject   predicate

A **compound sentence** combines two simple sentences, or independent clauses, with a comma and a conjunction such as *or, and,* or *but.*

<u>These towns</u> <u>used to be busy mining towns</u>, but <u>few people</u> <u>live there now</u>.
   subject   predicate   subject   predicate

Write **simple** or **compound** to show the type of sentence.

1. _____ Ghost towns can be found all around the United States.

2. _____ Some towns were just mining camps, but people still moved there.

3. _____ Men moved to these towns for the adventure of finding gold.

4. _____ The mines ran out of gold, and the miners left the towns.

5. _____ People still like to visit ghost towns today.

6. _____ Some ghost towns are parks, and the states protect them.

Circle the letters of the two simple sentences in each group of three. Then use a comma and the conjunction shown in parentheses to rewrite the two simple sentences as one compound sentence.

7. (and)   a.   A few men found gold.
           b.   While they were digging in the hills.
           c.   Other men came to find gold.

_____

_____

8. (but)   a.   Wanted to be rich.
           b.   Gold is what brought the men to the towns.
           c.   The gold soon ran out.

_____

_____

Pinknose

Editors must know that different kinds of sentences are correct.

A **simple sentence** is one **independent clause.** It has a subject and a predicate. It expresses a complete thought.

Pinknose is a chipmunk.

A **compound sentence** has two independent clauses.

Pinknose comes to the step, and he eats out of my hand.

A **complex sentence** has one independent clause and one or more dependent clauses. A **dependent clause** has a subject and predicate, but it is not a complete thought. The dependent clauses are underlined in these sentences.

Pinknose jumped <u>as he saw the cat in the yard</u>.

<u>As he saw the cat in the yard</u>, Pinknose jumped.

Write an **S** (simple), a **C** (compound), or a **CX** (complex) to show the kind of sentence.

_____ 1. Pinknose comes to our yard, and he gets treats.

_____ 2. Pinknose runs across the yard as he looks for food.

_____ 3. The squirrels chase Pinknose, and the neighbor's cat chases him, too.

_____ 4. Pinknose is faster than the squirrels or the cat!

_____ 5. As he runs, he watches for hiding places in the garden.

_____ 6. Pinknose darts into the ivy.

_____ 7. He peeks out from the leaves, and he waits patiently.

_____ 8. When he sees the cat leave the yard, Pinknose is off in a flash!

_____ 9. He jumps onto the porch, and he leaps onto my foot.

_____ 10. Pinknose begs for a piece of apple.

_____ 11. He also likes almonds, but he hates peanuts.

_____ 12. Pinknose stuffs his cheeks full of treats, and he runs back home again.

The Train Ride

Sometimes editors must fix run-on sentences. A **run-on sentence** is two or more sentences that run together without correct punctuation or a conjunction.

run-on: The train pulled into the station it stopped.

run-on: The train pulled into the station, it stopped.

Fix these run-on sentences by writing shorter sentences.

1. "All aboard!" the conductor yelled, he wore a blue suit.

   _____

   _____

2. Jessie stepped on board it was her first train ride.

   _____

   _____

3. She was nervous, she sat near a window.

   _____

   _____

Fix these run-on sentences by writing compound sentences. Remember to use a comma and a conjunction in each one.

4. Jessie felt the train move, she gasped out loud.

   _____

   _____

5. Soon, she saw farms and forests race by she gazed at the countryside.

   _____

   _____

6. Jessie held her carpetbag with both hands, she put her hat on the seat.

   _____

   _____

Rodeos

The **main idea** of a paragraph is called the **topic.** One sentence usually tells what the topic is. That sentence is called the **topic sentence.** The topic sentence is often the first one in the paragraph. An editor must make sure that the topic sentence tells the main idea clearly.

Read the paragraph. Then answer the questions.

The first rodeos started in the 1870s and 1880s. Ten years later, rodeos became yearly events. Today, many towns have rodeos. There are roping contests and horse racing. Cowboys enter bronco-busting and bull-riding events. Barrel racing is a special event for women. All of the riders use skills that they need for work on ranches. The fun and exciting rodeo has grown from its beginnings into the well-known sport it is today.

Circle the right answer.

1. The topic sentence of this paragraph is missing. What is the main idea of the passage?
   a. working on a ranch
   b. barrel racing
   c. summertime events
   d. the history of rodeos

2. Choose the best topic sentence for this paragraph.
   a. Another exciting sport is the chuck-wagon race.
   b. Rodeos began long ago when cowboys wanted to see who was the best at roping and riding.
   c. Cowboys are good riders.
   d. Roping is the most important skill for ranch work.

3. Write your own topic sentence for this paragraph. Be sure to use correct capitalization and punctuation.

   _____

   _____

4. Circle two details that could be added to this paragraph.

   the place where the first rodeo was held

   other Western sports

   how horses are trained

   how many towns today have rodeos

   why ranches are important

◆◆

In the Details

A **paragraph** is a group of sentences that tells the reader about one main idea.

This is a paragraph:

The **topic sentence** tells the main idea of a paragraph. Often, the topic sentence comes first. The rest of the sentences tell more about that idea. These are called **supporting sentences** or **details.** All of the sentences in a paragraph tell about one main idea.

Editors must make sure that topic sentences are supported by other sentences in the paragraph.

◆◆

Match the topic sentence with a supporting sentence that makes sense.

_____ 1.   People should visit my state.

_____ 2.   Many accidents happen to small children alone at home.

_____ 3.   I think you should read *Women of the Wild West.*

_____ 4.   Aunt Jenny's muffins are crisp on top and soft inside.

_____ 5.   Many teenagers have poor handwriting.

_____ 6.   Most students at our school do not like cooked vegetables.

_____ 7.   Tender Teddy is a soft and cuddly new toy.

_____ 8.   The Midville County Fair is a fun-filled time for everyone.

a.   He is the perfect pal for any toddler.

b.   That's why they should not be left alone in the home.

c.   It has many beautiful old buildings.

d.   Our cafeteria serves raw carrots and celery sticks.

e.   There are rides, games, and food-tasting contests.

f.   More handwriting lessons in elementary school would help.

g.   She is the best baker in the state!

h.   This book by Debbie Dillinger is about pioneer women.

Tornado!

A **topic sentence** tells the **main idea** in a paragraph. **Supporting sentences** explain more about the main idea. Editors must make sure that each topic is supported by details. A paragraph often includes at least three key supporting sentences.

Read each topic sentence. Then circle three sentences that support each topic.

1. Tornadoes form in storm clouds when warm air and cold air meet.
    a. They form when the two air masses come together.
    b. States in the Great Plains often have storms.
    c. Warm air rises from the ground, and the storm winds begin to swirl in the sky.
    d. A tornado is very dangerous.
    e. Tornadoes over water are called waterspouts.
    f. When the swirling wind reaches the ground, it is called a tornado.

2. Tornado Alley lies in the center of the United States.
    a. States with mountains do not have many tornadoes.
    b. Tornadoes can form quickly.
    c. The states in Tornado Alley have open, flat land and many storms.
    d. Tornadoes happen almost every year in this part of the country.
    e. A tornado watch means that the weather is right for a tornado to form.
    f. Texas, Oklahoma, Kansas, and Nebraska are all part of Tornado Alley.

3. A tornado came very close to our house last spring.
    a. The sky turned dark even though it was daytime.
    b. Weather forecasters do not know exactly when a tornado will happen.
    c. Tornadoes sound like trains.
    d. We could hear the wind roaring past our windows.
    e. My aunt once saw a tornado while she was driving.
    f. The high winds knocked down our neighbor's tree.

◆◆◆◆◆◆◆◆◆◆◆◆◆◆◆◆◆◆◆◆◆◆◆◆◆◆◆◆◆◆◆◆◆◆◆◆◆

A Famous Flight

A topic sentence tells the main idea in a paragraph. Supporting sentences explain more about the main idea. An editor makes sure that all of the supporting details help to explain the main idea.

◆◆◆◆◆◆◆◆◆◆◆◆◆◆◆◆◆◆◆◆◆◆◆◆◆◆◆◆◆◆◆◆◆◆◆◆◆

Read the paragraph. Then circle the right answer to each question.

(1) It might not seem so amazing today. (2) But Charles Lindbergh's flight to Paris was big news in 1927. (3) Another news story in 1927 was about an earthquake in China. (4) Nobody had ever flown a plane across the ocean. (5) People thought that planes were fun to watch. (6) They also thought that planes were unsafe. (7) Charles Lindbergh believed planes could play an important part in world transportation. (8) When he flew across the ocean, he proved that fact to others.

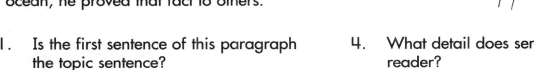

1. Is the first sentence of this paragraph the topic sentence?

    a. yes
    b. no

2. What is the topic of this paragraph?

    a. the danger of airplanes
    b. crossing the ocean
    c. Lindbergh's flight to Paris
    d. transportation

3. Why are sentences 5 and 6 included?

    a. to tell us that flying is fun
    b. to tell us what people of Lindbergh's time thought about airplanes
    c. to explain what airplanes are used for
    d. to explain that Charles Lindbergh was foolish

4. What detail does sentence 7 give the reader?

    a. that Lindbergh felt differently about airplanes than most people of his time
    b. that Lindbergh was not following safety rules of his time
    c. that Lindbergh was interested in many kinds of transportation
    d. that Lindbergh was a good pilot

5. Which sentence does not support the main idea?

    a. sentence 2
    b. sentence 3
    c. sentence 6
    d. sentence 7

6. If another paragraph followed this one, what do you think the topic would be?

    _____

    _____

Revolution

A paragraph is a group of sentences that tells the reader about one main idea. Remember that paragraphs follow a pattern:

The first line is indented.

The first sentence is usually the topic sentence.

The second, third, and fourth sentences support the topic sentence with details.

Read each paragraph. Cross out sentences that do not support the topic sentence.

1.   George Washington did not want to be a soldier. He loved being a planter. He was very happy running his farm. At one time, Washington was in the army. When he left the army, he said he would never go back. Martha Custis had two children. But his country needed him to help fight the British. Washington was not happy. But he did what he was asked to do. We are lucky that he did.

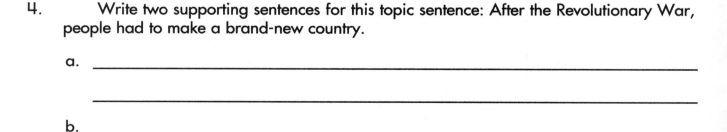

2.   The winter at Valley Forge in 1777 was a bad time in the war. Washington's soldiers were cold and hungry. Martha came to the camp to see her husband. They were happy to see each other. Washington tried to help his troops learn how to be better soldiers. And it was after that winter that the war began to go better for the Americans.

3.   Mount Vernon is the name of George Washington's home. He loved his farm. He tried growing new crops there. He added rooms to his house. He also liked dogs. He had one dog named Sweet Lips. Washington felt at peace when he was at Mount Vernon. After he retired, Washington went home to this peaceful place again.

4.   Write two supporting sentences for this topic sentence: After the Revolutionary War, people had to make a brand-new country.

    a. _____

      _____

    b. _____

      _____

 0-7424-2754-4 *Proofreading & Editing*

The Windy City

A paragraph is a group of sentences that tells the reader about one main idea. If sentences do not support the main idea, they do not belong in the paragraph. The editor must take these sentences out.

Read each paragraph. Circle the letter of the sentence following the paragraph that tells the main idea. Cross out one sentence in each paragraph that does not support the main idea.

1.   Most people know that Chicago is called the Windy City. People have many ideas about how this nickname came to be. Some say that a group of people bragged about the city. They did this to try to get Chicago picked as the place for the 1893 World's Fair. People in cities chose school boards, too. One newspaper said that people should not believe all of the claims about "that windy city." The *wind* meant bragging, not breezes! Now you know one reason Chicago is called the Windy City.

   a.   Chicago is called the Windy City because people bragged about it too much.

   b.   Editors who write about windy cities run their newspapers like businesses.

2.   Chicago is well known for its big fire. This fire burned down the city in 1871. It burned for three days. More than 90,000 people lost their homes. Fires are problems all over the world. Nobody knows exactly how the fire started. Some people think a cow kicked over a lantern. Then the lantern started a fire behind someone's house. This fire spread and grew into the huge fire that burned the city.

   a.   A cow started the great fire of 1871.

   b.   The great fire of 1871 burned down much of Chicago.

3.   Circle sentences that could belong in the second paragraph.

   a.   Cows should not be allowed in large cities.

   b.   Firefighters are very brave.

   c.   Chicago was rebuilt quickly.

   d.   A long dry spell helped the fire to spread quickly.

Dreams

A paragraph is a group of sentences that tells the reader about one main idea. It has a topic sentence and supporting sentences, and it may have an **ending,** or **concluding,** sentence. If there is no concluding sentence, the writer has more ideas to tell the reader.

The next paragraph starts with a new topic sentence. It has a **transition,** something that helps the reader know there is a new idea. Supporting sentences tell more about the new idea.

Only the last paragraph must have a **concluding sentence.** This final sentence should remind the reader about the topic.

Read the three-paragraph essay. The transitions are underlined for you. Find and underline the concluding sentence.

Long ago, people had many ideas about dreams. Some people said that if a person dreamed of the same thing three nights in a row, the dream would come true. Others thought that if a person said something about a dream before breakfast, it would bring bad luck.

However, in the last 100 years, dreams have become important in a different way. Doctors study dreams. They find that people who are troubled may dream about their problems. Sometimes the dream shows a way to solve the problem.

But we still have other beliefs about dreams, too. Have you ever been given a piece of wedding cake? An old proverb says that you should put the cake under your pillow. Then you'll dream about the person you will marry. All of these different ways of looking at dreams show that they are powerful and important.

Choose the transition word that fits each topic sentence.

1. _____ doctors thought that dreams were important in helping people.

   a. Intelligent
   b. Later,
   c. Older
   d. Modern

2. _____ many things about dreams are not known even though scientists continue to study dreams.

   a. Very
   b. I think
   c. But
   d. Sleepy

3. _____ what matters most is that students get enough sleep so they don't dream when they should be studying.

   a. Finally,
   b. I guess
   c. Sometimes
   d. Mom says

Name _____ Date _____

Margo on Stage

The topic sentence in a paragraph tells the main idea. Supporting sentences explain more about the main idea. One job of an editor is to make sure that the sentences are written in an order that makes sense.

1. The story below is mixed up. Read all of the sentences first.

    On the line, write a number 1 to show which sentence should come first. Number the other sentences to show their correct order. Underline the topic sentences of the paragraphs. (Hint: There are three paragraphs.)

    _____ She had play practice every night after school.

    _____ "We are so proud of you!" her parents said when they heard her news.

    _____ Margo was very nervous that evening because she had never been in front of an audience.

    _____ Margo chose to try out for the school play.

    _____ At the end of the play, the audience clapped and cheered.

    _____ Margo had to learn all of her lines by heart.

    _____ She was thrilled when she found out that she had a part!

    _____ But she felt better knowing that her family would be there to watch her on stage.

    _____ The play went very well.

    _____ At play practice, she also learned how to move on stage.

    _____ Margo knew she had made the right choice; her first play was a hit!

    _____ She ran all the way home to tell her parents the big news about her part.

    _____ The night of the play finally came.

2. Write another sentence that could be a part of this story.

    _____

    _____

Name _____ Date _____

Balloon Rocket

A paragraph is a group of sentences that tells the reader about one main idea. Editors must know where one paragraph ends and another starts. They also must make sure paragraphs are in an order that makes sense.

Read Ang's report about making a balloon rocket. In the blanks, number the paragraphs to show their correct order.

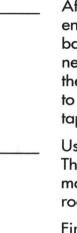

_____ After the string is set, blow up the balloon, but do not tie the end. Use the clothespin to hold the end closed. Place the balloon underneath the straw. Put the mouth of the balloon near the end of the straw. Use tape to hold the balloon to the straw. Be sure to blow up the balloon before you tape it to the straw. This will keep the balloon from pulling on the tape.

_____ Use the clothespin to seal the end of the blown-up balloon. Then use markers to decorate your rocket. Stripes or flags make great decorations. You might even want to name your rocket. Then get ready to fly!

_____ First, tie one end of the string to a doorknob. Next, slip the other end of the string through the straw. Tie it to the back of a chair. The string should be pulled tight. The straw should move easily along the string.

_____ Have you ever made a balloon rocket? It's easy. Before starting, you need these items: a long string, a drinking straw, a balloon, tape, a clothespin, and colored markers. Once you have everything, you are ready to start putting your rocket together.

_____ Your rocket is now ready to fly. If you were to let go of the end of the balloon, the air would rush out and push the rocket along the string. There's only step left: to decorate your rocket.

The Contest

A paragraph is a group of sentences that tells the reader about one main idea. Editors need to know where one paragraph ends and another starts. Editors use this mark to show the start of a new paragraph: ℙ. They use other proofreading marks (ℐ ∧ ≡ ∕ ∪) to fix other mistakes in the paragraphs.

Read this story. Use proofreading marks to fix the mistakes. Use the paragraph mark to show where each new paragraph begins.

many years ago, the winde and the sun fought about witch of them was stronger. Seeing a traveler coming there way, the sun said that they should have a kontest Whichever one could take away the traveler's cloak wood be named more powerful. The wind agreed, and the the

contest began. The wind went first. He puffed cold aire at the traveler. The wind blew and blue and blew. The harder he blew, the closer the traveler drew his cloak. The wind blew with all of his force, but the traveler held his cloak arownd him tighter still. Then it was the sun's tern. Gently, she beamed her warmth down onto the tired and cold traveler The sun's rays reeched the man, and he became very warm. The traveler smiled. He took of his cloak and carried it as he went on his way.

Focus on Paragraphs

A paragraph is a group of sentences that tells the reader about one main idea. Editors must look at many things when they proofread paragraphs. They must know the topic and see that it is supported by details. They must take out sentences that do not belong.

Read the paragraph. Circle the letter of the best topic sentence.

1. _____ . Most are in the highlands of the Southwest. The horses find it hard to get food during the winter months. Snow covers the grass that they feed on. Their numbers grow smaller each year.

   a. Horses have soft fur.
   b. Horses are interesting animals.
   c. About 20,000 wild horses live in our country.
   d. Horses can be ridden for work or for fun.

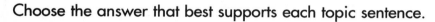

Choose the answer that best supports each topic sentence.

2. Birds eat many different things.

   a. Their colors vary from drab to colorful.
   b. Small birds generally eat seeds and insects.
   c. Even in cities, birds can survive.

3. Myths were sometimes used to explain natural events.

   a. Thunder was explained as the pounding of Thor's giant hammer.
   b. Athena was the goddess of wisdom.
   c. Zeus was the chief Greek god, and Hera was his wife.

4. During colonial days, there were no bathtubs or showers in houses.

   a. Colonial days were during the time that European people first settled in America.
   b. There weren't any cars either. People had to travel by horse.
   c. People today take lots of baths. In fact, some people even have swimming pools and hot tubs in their houses.
   d. Baths were not missed, though. People thought that baths were unhealthy!

Focus on Paragraphs (cont.)

5.   Read the paragraph. Choose the main idea of the paragraph.

What animal has four feet on the ground and its head in the clouds? It is a giraffe. The giraffe is the tallest mammal on Earth. At up to 19 feet tall, the giraffe towers above most animals. Some scientists think that other animals stay close to giraffes because giraffes can see danger coming from miles away.

a.   Many animals rely on the giraffe for protection.
b.   The giraffe eats more than most other African animals.
c.   The giraffe is an interesting mammal.

6.   Read the paragraph. Choose the best topic sentence for the paragraph.

_____ . Soap was once money to the people of Mexico. The people of England used lumps of coal as coins. People on the Pacific Ocean island of Yep used stone money. Even food has been used as money. In Russia, "coins" of cheese were used to buy things.

a.   Soap can be made from animal fat.
b.   Soap is often used to wash babies.
c.   Money was not always made of metal or paper, as it is today.
d.   Money has been around for a long time.

7.   Read the paragraph. Choose the sentence that does not belong.

(1) Rain is the biggest danger to baby birds. (2) During rainy weather, the parents still must leave the nest in search of food. (3) Baby birds usually eat chewed-up worms and bugs. (4) The baby birds are left uncovered. (5) The babies get chilled. (6) Thousands die during long rainstorms.

a.   sentence 1
b.   sentence 3
c.   sentence 4
d.   sentence 6

8.   Read the paragraph. Choose the sentence that fits best in the blank.

Today's cows give much more milk than cows of the past. _____ . Fifteen years ago, the average cow made just 6,000 quarts of milk. In ancient times, cows made only enough to feed their calves.

a.   Today, cows are much healthier.
b.   Milk has many vitamins that growing children need.
c.   Thanks to science, a modern cow makes 10,000 quarts of milk a year.

       0-7424-2754-4 Proofreading & Editing

Match Them Up

An editor must know the reason, or **purpose,** for writing. The editor must also know who the readers, or **audience,** will be. The title of a piece of writing tells a lot about the purpose and the audience.

Choose the best title for each audience and purpose.

1. **Audience:** your teacher and classmates
   Purpose: give a report about dolphins

   a. "Dolly the Magical Dolphin"
   b. "Dolphins: Friends in the Sea"
   c. "Life in the Ocean"

2. **Audience:** the math club
   Purpose: tell about the history of math discoveries

   a. "Math and Me"
   b. "Events That Add Up"
   c. "Great Moments in Math History"

3. **Audience:** a younger class
   Purpose: tell about books and reading

   a. "My First-Grade Teacher"
   b. "Books Are Great Friends"
   c. "My Favorite Book"

4. **Audience:** a class newsletter
   Purpose: give information on students' summer vacations

   a. "Our Class's Summer Stories"
   b. "What I Did on My Summer Vacation"
   c. "Why Vacations Are Important"

Now write titles for these pieces.

5. **Audience:** your teacher and classmates
   Purpose: tell a story about your most embarrassing moment

   _____

   _____

6. **Audience:** your mother
   Purpose: tell about your favorite memory of your mom

   _____

   _____

        0-7424-2754-4 *Proofreading & Editing*

The Right Topics

Before an editor starts to proofread, he or she must know the audience for a piece. The **audience** means the people who will be reading the piece of writing. An editor makes sure that the topic is written so it will interest the audience.

Choose the right answer to each question.

1. A book called *Power Tools for Home Repair* would interest—
   a. students in grade 2.
   b. kindergartners.
   c. homeowners.
   d. toddlers.

2. Choose the audience most interested in a book about how students should help care for their pets.
   a. newborn babies
   b. third graders
   c. cafeteria workers
   d. grocery store owners

3. The audience most interested in a speech called "Finding a Summer Job" would be—
   a. kindergartners.
   b. teenagers.
   c. grandparents.
   d. none of these

4. Choose the audience who would be most interested in a speech called "How to Do Magic Tricks."
   a. third graders
   b. fifth graders
   c. teenagers
   d. all of these

5. Miguel wants to write a letter to the newspaper about how more people need to recycle. Circle the best topic sentence.
   a. Recycling is simple and easy to do, so why aren't more people in our town recycling?
   b. Recycling is sorting your trash and sending it to centers to be used again.
   c. Recycling is important.

6. Tiffany is writing a story about her summer vacation. Circle the best first sentence.
   a. Summer vacations are important breaks for students.
   b. My cousin is going to Europe next year on her summer vacation.
   c. On the first day after school let out, I knew I was going to have a great summer vacation.

Name _____ Date _____

The Right Fit

An editor must know the reason, or purpose, for writing. The editor must also know who the readers, or audience, will be. If the writing doesn't match the audience, the editor needs to think of ways to make it fit better.

Match each topic sentence to the right audience and purpose.

_____ 1. For centuries, people have wondered about the secrets of the stone ring called Stonehenge.

_____ 2. My dog Buster is silly and friendly and the biggest eater in the whole state.

_____ 3. I could not stop reading *Tuck Everlasting* because I had to see if the characters' secret would be discovered.

_____ 4. Dear Diary: Today was one of the worst days of my life.

_____ 5. The red planet of Mars has been our neighbor and a mystery at the same time.

_____ 6. My math hero is a woman named Fan Chung Graham.

a. **Audience:** your teacher and classmates
Purpose: write a report about a planet

b. **Audience:** your teacher and classmates
Purpose: report on a famous world landmark

c. **Audience:** the book club
Purpose: report on a book you have read

d. **Audience:** yourself
Purpose: record your life in a diary

e. **Audience:** your teacher and classmates
Purpose: give a speech about your best friend

f. **Audience:** the math club newsletter
Purpose: write about a famous person in math history

Author Tour

An editor must know the purpose for writing. The editor must also know who the audience will be. If the writing doesn't match the audience, the editor thinks of ways to make it fit better. Sometimes the editor must take out sentences that don't fit the topic.

1. Edit Kara's report. Check the punctuation, spelling, and capitalization. Mark the paragraphs. Use proofreading marks to fix mistakes. You can use this mark to take out sentences that don't belong in the story: ~~My name is Kara.~~

My favorite athor is Laura ingalls Wilder, I have read everything she ever wrote. I have even tried some of her recipes! I also really like Paula danzinger's books. So, this past summer when my Parents said they where taking me on a tour of Laura's many homes, I was very happy We stopped at ant Mary's house. First, we went to Lake pepin, where Laura toore her dress as she put pebbles in her pockets. We saw walnut Groove her home near Plum Creek. Then we drove to De Smet, south Dakota. South Dakota is a big state. We saw the house where laura and her family lived when they first moved their We went to their homestead on the prairie. We got to see the Ingalls family home. Our last stop was in Missouri we visited Rocky Ridge Farm. This was where Laura livved after she married almanzo Wilder. There is a museum on the farm. It has things that belonged to Lara It was great to see Pa's fiddle Laura's books, and other things that are in her books.

2. Write the audience and the purpose for this essay.

Audience: _____

Purpose: _____

3. Write another sentence that Kara could put in her report.

_____

_____

Choose Your Words

Once you know your audience and your topics, you will be able to check vocabulary. Some words that are good to use in a letter to a friend are not the words you want to use in a report for school. Sometimes writers use the wrong word for a topic. An editor must choose words that will help the audience understand the writing.

Circle the best word to use in a piece of writing for each audience and purpose.

1. **Audience:** your teacher and classmates
   Purpose: give a report about animal homes

   a. cute
   b. cuddle
   c. habitat

2. **Audience:** the science club
   Purpose: tell about a discovery

   a. breakthrough
   b. bonus
   c. vacation

3. **Audience:** a younger class
   Purpose: give a speech about playground rules

   a. scientific
   b. study
   c. safety

4. **Audience:** a class newsletter
   Purpose: write about a class contest

   a. exit
   b. environment
   c. enter

5. **Audience:** computer game buyers
   Purpose: write an ad about a new game

   a. exciting
   b. crafts
   c. habitat

6. **Audience:** a letter to your grandparents
   Purpose: tell about your new baby sister

   a. tiny
   b. scientific
   c. environment

0-7423-2754-4 *Proofreading & Editing*

Choose Your Words (cont.)

Cross out the word that does not belong in each sentence. Use this mark: _____.
Then write a word on the line to replace the one you have taken out of the sentence.

7.   My baby brother is small, noisy, and invisible.

_____

8.   The steamy, freezing Amazon rain forest is the home of many animals.

_____

9.   The brave, high-tech explorers of North America came here throughout the 1600s.

_____

10.   Native Americans in the Northwest often grew totem poles.

_____

11.   Grandpa, do you remember when we stayed in that habitat on Lake Clare?

_____

12.   Name the fraction that is the answer to this cute equation.

_____

13.   Write a sentence that uses these words: *dinosaur, Ice Age, extinct.*

_____

_____

14.   Edit the incorrect words out of the beginning of this story. Add new words only if the sentences need them in order to be clear.

     Sierra walked back and forth at the end of the noisy blue pool. She had been practicing for months, and today she would have a chance to show off what she had

 learned about algebra. Just then Dana walked into the pool area. Sierra felt a rock in her throat. Dana was the second and only person she would have a hard time beating.

Name _____ Date _____

Careful Choices

Once you know your audience and your topics, you need to check vocabulary. Sometimes writers choose words that don't belong in a piece of writing. Sometimes a writer uses the wrong word. An editor must change it to a word that helps the audience understand the thought.

Read each paragraph. Then circle the word that could be used in another sentence added to the paragraph.

1. My friend told me about your community education classes. I have worked in a center like yours before. I helped make schedules. I also helped clean and handed out locker keys. Would you be interested in my help?

    a. restart
    b. review
    c. volunteer

2. Mr. Brockman is our art teacher. He asks students to help with jobs such as cleaning the paint brushes or passing out supplies. All of the students like helping in Mr. Brockman's class. Mr. Brockman changes our jobs every week so we all have a chance to do something we like.

    a. fair
    b. sad
    c. angry

3. Benjamin Franklin was born in 1706. He lived in Boston as a boy. Franklin had many jobs in his life. He was a famous writer. He started a library in Philadelphia. But we also remember him for his interest in science. He was interested in electricity, in flight, and in new ways to do things.

    a. firefighter
    b. experiments
    c. candlemaker

4. Our class's Good Citizen Award goes to someone who has helped many neighbors. Jamal Wheeler has spent the last year helping his neighbor, Mrs. Visconti, in her yard. He feeds people's pets when they go on vacation. He helped Mr. Anderson plant a vegetable garden. Jamal is a good example of what it means to be a neighbor.

    a. community
    b. responsible
    c. both a and b

5. Write a sentence describing a famous person in history. Be sure to use the right word choices in your description.

_____

_____

Words About Lincoln

Sometimes writers choose words that don't belong in a piece of writing, or they use the wrong word. An editor takes out words that don't fit and chooses words that help the audience understand the writing.

Read the essay. Use this mark to take out words that don't belong: _____.
Write a new word to replace the one that you take out.

Abraham Lincoln is respected by few people today. As our sixteenth President of the United States, Lincoln made selections that changed the lives of many Americans. His sense of fairness helped him guide the town through a terrible war.

One choice that Lincoln faced was about slavery. Lincoln believed that slavery was evil. He also believed that it did not move with the way in which the United States was set up. During the Civil War, President Lincoln carried a law freeing the slaves. Lincoln died in 1865, but his act became a building block for the past.

Lincoln was not perfect, but he was a man of honor. He thought that all people should be treated fairly. Because of his strong views, President Lincoln helped make our country an interesting place to live.

Choose the correct answer to each question.

1. In the first paragraph, which phrase would also fit?
   a. brave choices
   b. old buildings
   c. forgotten actions

2. In the second paragraph, which quotation would also fit?
   a. "Out of many, one."
   b. "All men are created equal."
   c. "Time flies."

3. In the third paragraph, which sentence would also fit?
   a. Lincoln was born in Kentucky.
   b. Lincoln worked as a lawyer at one time in his life.
   c. Lincoln is remembered for the good choices that he made.

Check Your Sources

When you proofread writing, sometimes you need to check **sources.** These are the places where the writer got information. An editor must make sure that facts, dates, and other information in the piece of writing are correct. The sources help the editor make sure that everything in the writing is correct.

Choose which source would help you the most to proofread and check each piece of writing.

1. a list of spelling words
   a. an atlas
   b. a dictionary
   c. a magazine article
   d. an encyclopedia

2. a report about the human body
   a. a dictionary
   b. Volume G of the encyclopedia
   c. Volume H of the encyclopedia
   d. an atlas

3. a book report
   a. a biography of the author
   b. a story about the same subject
   c. the library catalog listing of the book
   d. a book about illustrators

4. a class newspaper article about summer vacations
   a. student essays about their summer vacations
   b. a report about vacation time
   c. Volume S of the encyclopedia
   d. a mystery story set in the summer

5. a funny poem about strange words
   a. an encyclopedia, to check facts
   b. a dictionary, to check spellings and meanings
   c. *Martha Speaks*, about a dog who talks
   d. another poem about words

6. What sources can you think of to help you edit a report about Native-American tribes?

   _____

   _____

7. What sources could you use to help you edit a story about a family from Japan?

   _____

   _____

Spiders!

When you look at a piece of writing, sometimes you need to check sources. These are the places where the writer found information. An editor needs to make sure that facts, dates, and other details in the piece of writing are correct. The sources help the editor make sure that everything in the writing is correct.

Here is a list of facts from a book on spiders. Marta used this list to write her report.

Spider Facts

1. Spiders have eight legs.
2. Each leg has seven parts.
3. Each leg has two claws at the bottom.
4. Spiders have one to four pairs of eyes.
5. They use these eyes to see all around them.
6. A few types of spiders are blind.
7. Spiders have two main body parts, head and abdomen.
8. Spiders can run very fast.
9. They leap at their enemies.
10. Some spiders have fangs.
11. Poison in the fangs kills enemies.
12. One type of spider: raft spider
13. The raft spider has a raft for a home.
14. The raft spider's home is a raft made of twigs and leaves.
15. Another type of spider: trap-door spider
16. Trap-door spiders have underground homes.
17. They catch enemies in webs and traps.

Here is Marta's report. Underline any fact that does not match the information on the list.

    Spiders are very interesting. They have eight legs and two claws. Their bodies have two main parts: the head and the abdomen. They have from one to four pairs of eyes, but a few spiders cannot see at all. Spiders do not run very fast. Many spiders make webs, but some other spiders have different kinds of homes. The raft spider lives underground. It makes a nest from twigs and leaves.

          0-7424-2754-4 *Proofreading & Editing*

Runaway Elephant

An editor must make sure that facts, dates, and other details in a piece of writing are correct. Sources help the editor do this. Sometimes the editor must check two different sources. The sources may have different information.

At the Bentley Zoo, an African elephant was missing from its pen. A reporter talked to people who were there the day the elephant disappeared. Read the reports and answer the questions. Then read the newspaper article on page 59.

Source 1: Statement of Jan Walters

My name is Jan Walters. I was walking to the elephant pens to watch the feeding. I saw a group of people heading down a path. I followed the group. They led me to an elephant pen. I saw that the door was broken and was hanging open. The tracks led to the woods behind the zoo. The tracks were wet and fresh. I was sure that the elephant could not be far away. A zoo worker ran past me with a bucket of peanuts. She was calling, "Wrinkles! Wrinkles!"

Source 2: Statement of Armand Lee

My name is Armand Lee. I was visiting the zoo today. A big group of people were at the elephant pen at 2:00 P.M. Everyone seemed confused. The door to the elephant pen was open. Then I noticed tracks leading away from the pen. There were also peanuts on the ground. I could hear someone in the woods calling a name. I think it was Wriggles. Then I heard a snapping of branches. A gray trunk reached out from behind a tree toward a peanut. Two people who worked at the zoo ran toward the tree.

Write an answer to each question.

1. What time of day was the elephant missing from its pen?

   _____

2. What was the elephant's name?

   _____

3. How do you know which elephant name is the right one?

   _____

4. Why were there peanuts on the ground?

   _____

5. Where was the elephant hiding?

   _____

6. How did the elephant get out of the pen?

   _____

Runaway Elephant (cont.)

An elephant was missing from its pen in the Bentley Zoo. Here is the article that the reporter wrote using the information from page 58. Read the article. Underline any fact that does not match something that one of the visitors said.

Missing Elephant Scares Zoo Visitors

An African elephant named Wiggles was missing from its pen on Friday morning. People came to the pen to watch the elephant be fed. They saw that the door to the pen had been left open. Old tracks led to the woods, showing that the elephant had been missing for a long time.

One visitor, Armand Leep, said that he watched a zoo worker run into the woods with a bucket of peanuts. Maybe the smell of the peanuts worked. Zoo workers saw the elephant reaching from the woods to pick up a peanut. They were able to get the elephant to walk back to its pen.

Fix each sentence that you underlined. Rewrite each sentence with the right information from the visitors' stories.

7. _____

_____

_____

8. _____

_____

_____

9. _____

_____

_____

10. _____

_____

_____

Name _____   Date _____

Fishing With Nick

Nick had to write a book report about a hobby. He likes to go fishing with his dad. Last Christmas, his dad gave him a book about fly-fishing. Then Nick went to hear the author of the book speak.

Read the electronic catalog card for Nick's book. Read the article about the talk that Nick heard by the author. Then answer the questions on page 61.

Source 1: Card Catalog Entry

AUTHOR: Lyle, Richard
TITLE: Fly-fishing for beginners/Richard Lyle
PUBLISHER: New York: Smith and Company, 1998
DESCRIPT: 200 p.p.: 22 cm
NOTES: "A fireside book"
SUBJECTS: Fly-fishing
ADD TITLE: Fly-fishing for beginners
ISBN: 027268379
DYNIX #: 392312
Copy Details
LIBRARY: KDL-East Grand Rapids Branch
STATUS: on shelf
CALL NUMBER: 799.12 Lyo : 9/98

Source 2: Newspaper Article

Author Speaks to Book Club

Author Richard Lyle spent Saturday morning talking to a group of fly-fishing fans. The famous fishing expert met with the Townsend Book Club in a room at the library.

Mr. Lyle told the group about learning to fish in western Montana. "At first, I hated fly-fishing," the author said. "It was so hard to cast. I kept getting tangled up in my line. But one day, everything just worked for me. I've fished every day I could since then."

Book club members asked Mr. Lyle if he had any favorite places to fish. "I still love fishing in Montana," he said. "I like the Clark Fork River and the Bitterroot River." One member asked if he had any tips for beginners. Mr. Lyle laughed. "Just work on your casting. Don't give up too soon!" he said.

         0-7424-2754-4 *Proofreading & Editing*

Fishing With Nick (cont.)

Answer the questions about the two sources on page 60.

1. What is the title of Nick's fly-fishing book?

_____

2. How long is Nick's book?

_____

3. Where did Nick hear the author speak?

_____

4. What is the author's name?

_____

Here is Nick's book report. Underline any facts that do not match the facts in the two sources on page 60.

My favorite book is *Fly-Fishing for Beginners* by Rick Lyle. This book tells how to get started with this sport. Fly-fishing is hard, but Mr. Lyle has always loved it. He learned how to fish in eastern Montana. In the book, he gives advice on how to cast, how to choose flies, and how to pick a fishing spot. Mr. Lyle says that one of his favorite fishing rivers is the Gallatin River. My dad took me fishing there last year. It is in southern Montana. Fly-fishing is complicated, but Mr. Lyle makes you believe that it is easy and fun. I think anyone who likes fishing should read this book.

Fix each sentence that you underlined. Rewrite each sentence with the correct information from the two sources.

5. _____

6. _____

7. _____

8. _____

The Iroquois

An editor must make sure that facts, dates, and other details in a piece of writing are correct. Sources help the editor make sure that everything in the writing is correct. Sometimes the editor must check three different sources. The sources may have different information.

Hannah wrote a report on the Iroquois tribe for her social studies class. She found three sources. Read the sources and then answer the questions on page 63.

Source 1: Article from *North American Tribes*

Native-American Life in the Northeast

Before Europeans came to the Northeast, thick forests covered the land. The Native Americans made these forests their homes. These tribes included the Iroquois, the Wampanoag, and the Mahicans.

During the winter, the Native Americans stayed close to home. They told stories, played games, and lived off the food they had gathered. As the weather warmed, they fished in rivers and streams. They gathered eggs and hunted geese.

In the spring, the Native Americans planted corn, beans, and pumpkins. They gathered wild fruit, herbs, and tree bark. They used some of these for medicines.

August was a time of harvest. The Native Americans would leave their villages to hunt in the woods. The men hunted for bear, deer, and other game. The meat was dried and saved for the cold winter months. The villagers came home at the first sign of snow. The Native Americans gave thanks for the food and shelter they had gotten from the forest.

Source 2: Chart

Iroquois Life

Food	game, fish, corn, beans, pumpkins
Shelter	wigwams, longhouses
Land	present-day New York
Clothing	shirts, leggings or skirts, moccasins
Language	Algonquin

Source 3: Magazine Article

Iroquois Games and Crafts

We don't often think about Native Americans enjoying themselves. But many tribes made time for fun as well as for work. The Iroquois are famous for one game that they invented: lacrosse. Their version of this game is like the one that is still played today. This tribe was also famous for its storytellers. Storytelling in the longhouses was enjoyed in the long, dark winter evenings. Another important part of Iroquois life was beadwork. The beautiful bead designs created by the Iroquois can be seen in museums today. These gifted people loved to make beadwork birds and flowers. These decorated their clothing and bags.

                             0-7424-2754-4 *Proofreading & Editing*

The Iroquois (cont.)

Answer the questions about the sources on page 62.

1. Which source will be most helpful to Hannah when she writes a report on the food, clothing, and shelter of the Iroquois?

   a. source 1
   b. source 2
   c. source 3

2. What must Hannah think about carefully as she uses source 1?

   a. The article does not talk about food gathering.
   b. The article describes more tribes than just the Iroquois.
   c. The article does not show how life was linked to the seasons.

3. If Hannah's report is supposed to be about food, clothing, and shelter, which source will she use the least?

   a. source 1
   b. source 2
   c. source 3

4. Here is a sentence from Hannah's report:

   The Iroquois gathered fruit and herbs from the forest.

   What might be wrong with this sentence?

   a. The Iroquois gathered fruit, but not herbs.
   b. Hannah must check to see what kinds of fruits and herbs grew in New York.
   c. Hannah must check to see if the Iroquois, and not just other tribes, did this.

5. Here is a section from Hannah's report:

   The Iroquois wore shirts, skirts or leggings, and moccasins. They decorated some of their clothing with beadwork that is famous today. They liked to use flowers and birds in their beadwork.

   Which two sources did Hannah use to write this part of her report?

   a. sources 1 and 2
   b. sources 2 and 3
   c. sources 1 and 3

6. Write two sentences about the homes of the Iroquois. Use the sources on page 62. Be sure to use correct spelling, punctuation, and grammar.

   _____

   _____

   _____

Check It Out!

A **checklist** is a tool. It is a list of items to edit in a piece of writing. This tool helps the writer find mistakes. Some mistakes, such as spelling errors, are in all types of writing. Other mistakes are only in some types of writing.

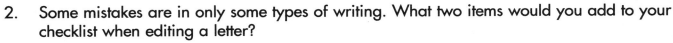

Read each question. Circle the correct answer or answers.

1. Which items would you edit in *everything* you write?

    a. spelling
    b. punctuation
    c. capitalization
    d. word choice
    e. clarity
    f. indenting
    g. extra or missing words
    h. fits audience and purpose

2. Some mistakes are in only some types of writing. What two items would you add to your checklist when editing a letter?

    a. no missing steps
    b. commas after the greeting and closing
    c. steps in the correct order
    d. comma between date and year

3. Which item would *not* appear on a checklist for instructions?

    a. steps in the correct order
    b. capitalize the first letter of each line
    c. no missing steps
    d. punctuation

4. Which items would you find on a checklist for a story?

    a. capitalization
    b. quotation marks
    c. all steps in the correct order
    d. end marks
    e. spelling
    f. comma after the greeting

5. Which items would be important to check in a report?

    a. report matches sources
    b. topic and supporting sentences
    c. commas after the greeting and closing
    d. clarity

Check It Out! (cont.)

Read the piece of writing. Use the checklist to edit. Use proofreading marks to fix the mistakes. Then answer the questions that follow. More than one correct answer is possible.

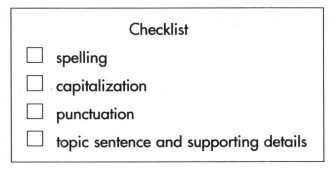

Checklist

- ☐ spelling
- ☐ capitalization
- ☐ punctuation
- ☐ topic sentence and supporting details

      Last summer, my family and I visited Mount Rushmore in South Dakota. The faces of four american presidents our carved into the rock up high on a mountin. At first, the faces didn't look very large. When we moved closer to them, we saw that they were huge! Mount rushmore is amazing

6. Which error is found using the checklist above?

   a. Last summer, my family and I visited Mount Rushmore in South Dakota.
   b. american
   c. mountin
   d. Mount rushmore

7. What other errors should be checked in this report?

   a. end marks
   b. comma after greeting
   c. homophones
   d. steps in correct order

8. Use the checklist to edit this start of a story.

Checklist

- ☐ spelling
- ☐ capitalization
- ☐ punctuation

      "Mother, come quickly! called anna. "It's Jacob! Hi's hurt!"

      Even though I new mother was hurrying, i was scared. Jacob's leg was bent in a strang way.

      "jacob? Mother tried to speak to him. "I'm here, Jacob. can you hear me?

Have a Heart!

A checklist helps when you edit a piece of writing. A checklist for a letter is special. The list has more items. One comma follows the greeting. One comma follows the closing. A comma also goes between the date and year.

1. Use the checklist to edit the letter.

Checklist

☐ spelling   ☐ comma between date and year
☐ capitalization   ☐ comma after greeting and closing
☐ punctuation   ☐ indenting

May 5 2005

Deer Monique

    Greetings! This letter is from your hart. I am speeking for all of your body parts. I know you don't usually get letters from us and you're probly surprised write now.

    There's something importint I'd like to tell to you I had a grate time on the hike you taked last weekend I pumped and thumped the whole way. You may not realize it, but all of the body parts liked it. It felt good to get all that bloood flowing. Lets make a promise to one anuther; if you keep working for us, we'll keep working for you! Thanks for the fantastic workout

Love,

You're very own heart

Circle the correct answer or answers.

2. This letter should be edited for—
   a. commas in a series
   b. comma between date and year
   c. homophones
   d. commas after the greeting and closing

3. What does not need to be edited in a letter?
   a. spelling
   b. word choice
   c. capitals in the title
   d. punctuation

     66   0-7424-2754-4 *Proofreading & Editing*

Name _____ Date _____

Did I Really Win?

A checklist for a letter is special. The list has more items. Look through the letter for each item on the checklist.

Use the checklist to edit this letter. Use proofreading marks to fix the mistakes.

Checklist

- ☐ spelling
- ☐ capitalization
- ☐ punctuation
- ☐ comma between date and year
- ☐ commas after greeting and closing
- ☐ indenting

October 18 2004

Dear **Reggie**

Congratulations! You may have alraedy won a lifetime supply of Bubble Trouble! Keep reeading to find out how your can claim your prize.

As you know, bubble trouble is sweeping the the nation. This delicious bubble gum lastes all day. Also though every piece of gum looks the same, each peice will turned your teeth a different color Just think of of the jokes you can play on your friends! But, **Reggie**, you may wonder how you can claim such a great prize. There are nine Bubble Truuble colors plus one bonus color. You must take. Pictures of eich color on your teeth. Then send in your photos along with you $4.95 entry fee. You will then, be in the drawing for a liftime supply of Bubble Trouble!

Happy chewing, **reggie**! We cant wiat to deliver your priz!

Sincerly

Mr Bubble Trouble

Think about it! In the first paragraph, the letter says that Reggie "may have already won a lifetime supply of Bubble Trouble!" Is it possible that he already won? How do you know?

Colorful Nome

A checklist for a letter is special. The list has more items. Look through the letter for each item on the checklist.

Use the checklist to edit the letter. Use proofreading marks to fix the mistakes. Check off each item as you edit it.

Checklist

- ☐ spelling
- ☐ capitalization
- ☐ punctuation

- ☐ comma between date and year
- ☐ commas after greeting and closing
- ☐ indenting

March 18 2004

Dear Rosa,

     Thank you for your letter and the gorgeous picture! It really maded me smile. I remember how beutiful the texas flours are in the Spring. The bluebonnets turn the hole hillside into a blue carpet! It's not as colorful here. we have three feet of snow on the grownd. The peple are colorful, though No one here worrys about fashion like they did in texas. They just get dressed every morning for whatevr the weather will bring. Their are som things I love about Texas. There are uther things I love about nome, alaska. The very best part about Texas, though, is you I miss you alot! Please write back.

Freinds always

Jeanne marie

1. The three paragraphs in this letter cover what basic topics?
   a. wildflowers, no flowers, missing flowers
   b. snow and ice, fashion in Nome, loving Nome
   c. Rosa's picture, fashion in Nome, loving Nome
   d. Rosa's letter and picture, life in Nome, missing Rosa

2. Check your editing of Jeanne Marie's letter for three new paragraphs. Use the paragraph mark to show where each new paragraph should begin.

Ice Lanterns

A checklist is a good tool to help you edit a piece of writing. Check off each item on the checklist as you edit for it. A checklist for instructions has a few extra items. All of the steps must be in the instructions. The steps must be in the right order.

1. Use the checklist to edit this letter. Use proofreading marks to fix the mistakes.

> ### Checklist
>
> ☐ spelling
> ☐ capitalization
> ☐ punctuation
> ☐ extra or missing words
>
> ☐ commas after transition words (*first, next, then, last*)
> ☐ all steps included
> ☐ steps in the correct order

Ice lanterns began in in Finland during the freeezing winters. You can makes your own ice lantern. you will need a large plastick bucket, a column candle water, and 0°F (−18°C) or colder wether.

First fill the bucket with water Put them outdoors overnight. the water will freeze around the edges and on the top. The ice shud be about two inchs thick.

Next, turn the buckit upside down. The water that did not freeze will spill off, the ice on the the bottom and sides of your lantren will stay. If the water freezed on the botom of the bucket, it will know be on top. Break it to find the hollow area in the ice.

The hollow part is a perfect place for a candle to glow in the dark

enjoy your new lantern!

2. What might happen if the weather is too cold?

_____

3. What step was left off this list?
    a. Place the water in the bucket outside.
    b. Turn the bucket upside down.
    c. Place the candle inside the lantern and light it.
    d. Break the ice on top of the lantern to find the hollow space inside.

Batting a Thousand

A writer often writes to explain something. The editor's job is to make sure the information is clear and correct. The details must be in order.

Read the following explanation. Then answer the questions on page 71.

Batting a thousand

(1)   Did you ever hear anyone say, "Your batting a thousand?" do you know where the saying comes from or what it means The first part of the qestion is easy to figure out. The word *batting* sounds as though it comes from baseball. It dose! But even if you play baseball, you might not undrstand the saying.

(2)   To understand the saying, you need to no more abowt baseball. Each time a batter gos to bat, she might get a hit or she might not. If the batter gits a hit most of the time, she is a very good batter. The best weigh to know if a batter is good is to look at her battinng average

(3)   Here is an example. Toni has been to bat ten times. She had for hits. Divid the number of hits by the number of tries. That's the batting average. For Toni's average, divide four by ten. Then put the anser into decimal form. Your answer should be 0.400. X So, 0.400 becomes 400. If you had not seen Toni play but new her batting average was 400, you would know she gets four hits in ten tries.

(4)   The batting average tells who good a batter is. It is a number that tells how meny times a batter gets a hit. How do you fined a batting average All you do is divide.

(5)   Now what about the saying? Toni was batting 400 by gitting four hits out of ten tries what if Toni were batting 1,000? Move the decimal back to the leff three places. This means that if you divide her hits by her tries, you get 1.000. The only way that happens is if she hits the ball every time. In baseball, batting a thousand meeans you always hit the ball. So, when someone says, "you're batting a thousand," it means you're doin very well.

70   0-7424-2754-4 *Proofreading & Editing*

Batting a Thousand (cont.)

Answer the questions about the explanation on page 70.

1. Writing should always be clear and complete. What sentence should be put in at the X to make the writing clear and complete?

   a. In math, 0.400 is the same thing as 400.
   b. Basebali is our favorite sport.
   c. In baseball, the decimal point is moved three places to the right.
   d. Ignore the extra zeros.

2. What is the topic sentence of paragraph 4?

   a. The batting average tells how good a batter is.
   b. It is a number that tells how many times a batter gets a hit.
   c. How do you find a batting average?
   d. All you do is divide.

3. Paragraph 4 does not seem to be in the right place. Where does it belong?

   a. before paragraph 1
   b. between paragraphs 1 and 2
   c. between paragraphs 2 and 3
   d. after paragraph 5

4. Use the checklist below to edit the explanation on page 70.

   Checklist

   ☐ spelling   ☐ clear and correct details

   ☐ capitalization   ☐ details in the correct order

   ☐ punctuation

5. "Batting a thousand" means you're doing very well. What would *batting zero* mean?

   a. You're doing fine.
   b. You're hitting the ball every time.
   c. You're doing poorly.
   d. You're hitting the ball every other time.

6. If a batter has an average of 700, how many times does he or she hit the ball out of ten tries?

The Greatest Invention

Reports give information. They must be clear and correct. The report must make sense to the reader. Each paragraph should have a clear main idea or topic sentence. The other sentences should support the main idea.

Read this report. Look for the main ideas and details. Then, answer the questions on page 73.

The Greatest Invention

Of all creatures on erth, only one has created music. A birds song may be beautiful, but the bird canot change it. The chirping of crickets may soothe us but it cannot stir the hart. The music of the human race can soothe chanje, and stir. Music is our greatest invention.

nothing touches people the way music can. Music can create. tears or similes on the faces of those who here it. A melody can tames a wild crowd. A daring song gives kourage to soldiers going into battle. simple drums can make people dance. From lullabies to marches, music is a part of life.

Music goes along with every event in people's lives. Weddings and birthdays have speshul songs. Baseball Fans sing a song for the sevinth inning stretch. county fairs and downtown malls offer some form of music. A dentist's office might play music to makes people feel better. Vets play soft music to ceep the pets calm. Whether people are working or playing. Music is somewhere nearby. And, where their is music, there is a chance to tuch someones heart.

The Greatest Invention (cont.)

1. Use this checklist to edit the report on page 72.

    ### Checklist

    ☐ spelling   ☐ topic sentences and supporting details
    ☐ capitalization   ☐ indenting
    ☐ punctuation   ☐ clear and correct details
    ☐ subject-verb agreement

2. Word choice is important in all types of writing. In reports, many people use the same word over and over. Find the words in this report that mean *music*. On the lines below, write as many as you can find.

    _____   _____

    _____   _____

    _____   _____

    _____   _____

3. In the third paragraph, the word "vets" is an abbreviation. Which word is the whole word?
    a. veterans
    b. vetchlings
    c. veterinarians
    d. vetoes

4. How do you know which word is the right one?

    _____

    _____

5. Why does the report say that music is our greatest invention?

    _____

    _____

6. What is the topic sentence in the second paragraph?
    a. Nothing touches people the way music can.
    b. Music can create tears or smiles on the faces of those who hear it.
    c. A melody can tame a wild crowd.
    d. From lullabies to marches, music is a part of life.

Wolves!

Writers give information in reports. Reports must be clear and correct. Facts used must be true and clear. The facts in the report must match the facts in the source, the place where the writer found the information.

Read the following report and the sources. Then answer the questions on page 75.

What Big, bad Wolf?

Little Red Ridding Hood and the Three Little Pigs may tell you that wolfs are not to be trusted. They might say that wolves are terible creatures that kill for fun. Leading wolf experts will tell you the fiary tales are wronge. The World wildlife defense group (WWDG) has studied wolves. They claim that wolves are not monstres from fairy tales. Instead, they beleive that people have caused problems for wolves. "Humans have taken over many wolf hunting grounds. now there is not enuf land to feed the wolves," the group's report says. Say the hunting ground for a pac of wolves changes into a pasture for sheep. how can people think the wolves to stay away? Elio gray agrees. This famus wolf expert explians that wolves do not normally hunt large animals such as cows or horses. "small birds rabbits deer, or sheep are the wolf's favorite foods. He says that wolves hunt on farms becuse thats where they used to hunt.

It seems clear that wolves are just trying to stay alive. Sometimes they may hunt on a farm or near a town. does that mean the wolf is as scary as the fairy tales tell us Or have we taken too much away from this noble animal?

Source 1: Quote from *Where Are the Wild Wolves?* by Elio Gray

"Wolves normally hunt small game. Birds, rabbits, and other small animals are the wolf's favorite foods. Sometimes a wolf pack will hunt a larger animal such as a deer or a sheep. But these larger animals are not the main source of food for wolves."

Wolves! (cont.)

Source 2: A report by the World Wildlife Defense Group (WWDG)

The gray wolf and the red wolf are both endangered. Humans have taken over many wolf hunting grounds. Now there is not enough land to feed the wolves. Many people think that wolves are wild killers. They think that wolves hunt people and livestock for fun. Sometimes wolves will hunt farm animals. But there are no known reports of wolves hunting humans. Wolves prefer to avoid humans.

1. Elio Gray is a wolf expert. Is there anything in the report that does not match the quote from his book?
   a. Yes. "This famous wolf expert explains that wolves do not normally hunt large animals such as cows or horses."
   b. Yes. "Small birds, rabbits, deer, or sheep are the wolf's favorite foods."
   c. Yes. "He says that wolves hunt on farms because that's where they used to hunt."
   d. No. The information in the report matches the quote from his book.

2. What is the main idea of this report?
   a. Wolves only hunt animals to survive.
   b. Wolves hunt large animals such as cows or horses.
   c. Wolves are terrible creatures that kill for fun.
   d. People expect wolves not to hunt for farm animals.

3. Write two sentences from the report that support the main idea.

   _____

   _____

   _____

4. Reread the report. Use the checklist below to edit the report. Use the sources to check the facts. Use proofreading marks to fix the mistakes.

   ### Checklist

   ☐ spelling   ☐ topic sentences and supporting details

   ☐ capitalization   ☐ indenting

   ☐ punctuation   ☐ clear and correct details

   ☐ subject-verb agreement   ☐ facts match the source material

Water, Water Everywhere

Reports give information, so they must be clear and correct. The facts in the report must match the facts in the source.

Read the report and the sources. Then answer the questions on page 77.

Water for Life
An Oral Report by Jason Hoo

For my classroom report, I will tell you about water. I wasn't very happy when Miss aegis gave me my topic. It sounded pretty boring to me. Now that Ive prepared my report, I can tell you that I learned a lot. let me give you a few facts.

Did you know that water helps your hole body work right? Water makes every organ every joint, and every cell of your body function. I learned that we even need water to dijest our foods. Although water doesn't have any nutrition in it, you should drink water every day. How much water do you need When I did my reserch, it said ate to ten cups for most people. nate, since you exercise so much and run those long races, you don't neeed as much water as the rest of us. The best way to get water is at the drinking fountain. Drinking fuontains are fun! The more you drink, the happier you're body will be. You can also get water threw some foods. Make sure you eat lots of fruit! If you give your body the water it needs, you'll be healthier.

Source 1: TV interview with Dr. I. M. Thirsty

"Water is very important to our health. Water helps the blood carry oxygen and nutrients to our cells. It also helps to flush wastes out of our bodies. Our joints and soft tissues, such as skin and organs, rely on water to function. Water keeps a good balance between the salts and fluids in our cells. We even need water to help us digest foods and absorb nutrition. Water may be the key to our daily health."

Source 2: from "Water" in the encyclopedia

"The human body is over 60 percent water. As the body uses this water, it must have a new supply throughout the day. Most people need 8 to 10 cups of water each day. An athlete needs more. Drinking is the best source. Water can also be gotten from foods such as fruit, meat, and some grains."

Water, Water Everywhere (cont.)

Circle the correct answer to each question.

1. There is a detail in Jason's report that is not correct. What is the detail?

   a. Water makes every cell of your body function.
   b. You can also get water through some foods.
   c. Nate, you don't need as much water as the rest of us.
   d. You should drink water every day.

2. What detail from the interview did Jason leave out of his report?

   a. Water is very important to our health.
   b. We even need water to help us digest foods.
   c. It also helps to flush wastes out of our bodies.
   d. Our joints, skin, and organs need water to function.

3. What sentence is not appropriate for this report?

   a. Did you know that water helps your whole body work right?
   b. I wasn't very happy when Miss Aegis gave me my topic.
   c. I learned that we even need water to digest our foods.
   d. The best way to get water is at the drinking fountain.

4. What is the main idea of the last paragraph?

   a. People need 8 to 10 cups of water a day.
   b. The best way to get water is at the drinking fountain.
   c. Water helps the whole body work better.
   d. Be sure to get the water your body needs.

5. Write one detail from the paragraph that supports that main idea.

   _____

6. Write one detail from the paragraph that does not support that main idea.

   _____

7. Reread the report. Use the checklist below to edit the report. Use proofreading marks to fix the mistakes.

Checklist

☐ spelling
☐ capitalization
☐ punctuation
☐ subject-verb agreement

☐ topic sentences and supporting details
☐ indenting
☐ clear and correct details
☐ facts match the source material

A Historic Birthday Party

Reports give information, so they must be clear and correct. Writers must check the facts that they use. The facts in a report must match the facts in the sources.

Read the report and the sources. Then follow the instructions on page 79.

A Historic Birthday Party

River City is 150 years old! mayor Sam Fenn III will threw a grand party in the park. The birthday party will be this sunday at four o'clock. The whole town is invited. Over 45,000 poeple may attend!

This party will be the bigger ever in river city. Rock and country bands will play in the park. Shop owners will have food drinks, and T-shirts for sail. There will even be fun rides for kids.

Is this year's party like parties in the past? Take a trip through histry! Fifty years ago, the party would has been for fewer than 20,000 people. mayor Joyce Hill would have hosted the party. There was no rock music then. The only ride was a pony ride.

One hundred year ago, Samuel Fenn went to the last town party of he's life. Fiddlers played in the town scuare for 1,000 people. The main fun was the square dance.

In 1883 they didn't want to have a party. In 1873 they had a party in the new town hall. In 1853, they din't even know they were starting a town.

The parties have groan through the years The music and the mayors have changed. even the food and games are different. As the town turns 150 years old, rember the past. Its what makes River City so special.

Source 1: River City Timeline

Town Founded	First Town Hall	Great River Flood	Death of Founder Samuel Fenn	Fenn Furniture Factory Opens	First Traffic Light	Sammy Fenn III Elected Mayor
1853	1872	1882	1904	1947	1970	1995

　　　　78　　　　0-7424-2754-4 *Proofreading & Editing*

A Historic Birthday Party (cont.)

Source 2: Article from *The River City News*

One hundred and fifty years ago, Samuel J. Fenn rode down from Rocky Top Hill. He led a team of young men toward their dreams of gold in California. Samuel Fenn climbed down from his mule and set his pack on the open ground. He and his followers set up camp. They were only supposed to stay for a couple of weeks to hunt for food. They said they needed a rest before crossing the mountains. Instead, they stayed. The rest, as they say, is history.

Source 3: Population Chart for River City

Year	River City Population
1853	23 (estimate)
1863	385 (estimate)
1873	1,443 (estimate)
1883	842
1903	1,393
1923	5,614
1943	11,008
1953	18,111
1983	31,941
2003	48,730

1. Why would the people of River City not want to celebrate in 1883? (Use your sources to find the answer.)

_____

2. In 1853, why didn't the people know they were founding a town?

_____

3. Reread the report. Use the checklist to help you edit the report. Use proofreading marks to fix the mistakes.

Checklist

- ☐ spelling
- ☐ capitalization
- ☐ punctuation
- ☐ subject-verb agreement
- ☐ topic sentences and supporting details
- ☐ indenting
- ☐ clear and correct details
- ☐ facts match the source material

    79

Treasure!

A writer uses a checklist to edit a piece of writing. A story is a special type of writing. It needs a **beginning,** a **middle,** and an **end.** The setting, the characters, and a problem appear in the beginning of a story. Events happen in the middle of a story. The problem is solved near the end of the story. Look for these parts in this story.

Read the story. Then answer the questions on page 81.

Treasure!

Captain gomez pointed his ship north. He keeped the coast of Africa far to one side. his crew and his ship lef the Ivory Coast without ivory or gold. In fact their ship had no cargo. Captain Gomez carried a a better treasure. He brung news four his king. But the news was olny good if he got it to the king quickly. calm winds had slowed his trip for two days already. Now his ship was in waters that were home to many Pirates. of course, without the wind, the pirates' ships would be as slow as his.

On the third day, two other ships were sighted to the north Captain Gomez knew that if they were pirate ships, they could cut off his escape. The time passed slowlier as the three drifting ships wached each other from afar. Finally the winds began to blow Captain Gomez smiled.

The sails filled and pushed the ship ofer the water. When he got closer, he saw that thay both flew pirate flags. The winds were with Captain Gomez that day His empty ship was able to sial past the heavier pirate ships. They couldn't catch him.

Captain Gomez sailed arownd the north end of africa. It wasn't not long before he was home. He went to his king. Eagerly he shared his news. He had found a new french trade route. the king gave the Captain his own treasure as a reward.

Treasure! (cont.)

Answer these questions about the story on page 80. Reread the story to find the answers.

1. What is the setting (time and place) in which the story takes place?

    _____

2. Who are the characters in the story?

    _____

    _____

3. What is the problem in the story? What keeps the main character from getting what he wants?

    _____

    _____

4. What happens in the middle of the story?

    _____

    _____

5. How is the problem solved at the end of the story?

    _____

    _____

6. What was the "treasure" that Captain Gomez had found?

    _____

    _____

7. Go back and edit the story using the following checklist. Use proofreading marks to fix the mistakes.

    Checklist
    - ☐ spelling
    - ☐ capitalization
    - ☐ punctuation
    - ☐ subject-verb agreement
    - ☐ story elements (beginning, middle, end)
    - ☐ indenting

Caught in a Cave!

When you edit a story, check for quotation marks when a character speaks. Look for a beginning, a middle, and an end of the story. Begin a new paragraph when a new idea begins or someone different speaks.

Read the story. Then answer the questions on page 83.

Caught in a Cave!

"What else can go wrong with your cave trip" asked joAnn, panting for air. Lee was too busy gasping and coughing to answer. The to cave explorers found themselves in a small room filled with water They lifted their faces up into the air poket. their noses scraped the ceiling as they took in the air. Already on this trip, thay had smashed a lamp. With only one lamp left, they moved slowly through the caves. Then they had snapped a rope. when the rope broke, they had dropped ten feet into the water-filled room. They had to find a new way out. "Dont worry, said Lee. "I feel a breeze in this room. The water has to show the way out somewear. I will find it."

"I'm not worried about the water getting out, lee!" cried JoAnn. Her voice began to crack. I'm worried about *us* getting out. Besides, you don't no where the next air gap will be." "I'll know in a minute" said Lee. She pulled her heead under the water, planted her feet against the ceiling and push herself down into the water. JoAnn waited in the pitch black. She listened to the sound of the water sloshing against the rock. She tried to push bak her tears, but she couldn't. How long had Lee been goen? was she coming back? JoAnn shrieked as a hand poped up next to her. It hit the rocky ceiling. Lee gulped the life-giving air. once she had her breath again, she told JoAnn what she had seen.

There's a passage halfway down that wall," Lee poynted her thumb past JoAnn. "It slopes up. I found another pocket of air not too far away. From there, I could saw some light. Maybe that means there's a weigh out of here.

Caught in a Cave! (cont.)

1. Reread the cave story. Mark where each new paragraph should begin.

2. Use the following checklist to edit this story. Use proofreading marks to fix the mistakes.

Checklist
☐ spelling
☐ capitalization
☐ punctuation
☐ subject-verb agreement
☐ story elements (beginning, middle, end)
☐ indenting

3. What is missing from this story? (Hint: A story includes a solution to the main character's problem.)
    a. beginning
    b. setting
    c. end
    d. characters

4. Finish the story on the lines below.

_____

_____

_____

_____

_____

_____

_____

The Uncertain Trail

Sometimes stories are written in journal form. In journal entries, one special task is to check that the dates have correct punctuation. This journal is a part of a story. The beginning, middle, or ending may not be complete.

Read the story. Then answer the questions on page 85.

April 10 1849

Five days west of missouri

I'll send this journal to Mama when we git to Oregon. I want her to know what the journey was like. The trail master sayed it will take us six months. Six months in a wagon dosn't sound too good to me. I know that Mama is alredy worried about me. She does seem happy that I am married, though. benjamin is sure that he can make a better life for us in Oregon. He says they'res free land for farmers. I hope hes right.

april 13, 149

Somewhere in the Grate American Desert

Id heared talk of the Great american Desert. It's amazing to see. We'll travel along the platte river next month. for now we carry most of our water. As far as I can see, there are just flat grassy lands I can't imagine people living here. The trail master says we don't need to worry abowt other people yet. After we pass Fort Kearny, he'll post more watches and send scouts ahead of the wagon train that kind of talk scares me.

April 19 1849

Still in the Great american Desert

I haven't writen in several days because nothing has changed. Every day is the same. The scenery never change from wide, flat plains. I pictured tall mountains. I thought there would be praries full of wildflowers I hope somethin changes soon. this journey is only two weeks old. all ready I am tired.

The Uncertain Trail (cont.)

1. Use the following checklist to edit the journal-style story on page 84.

Checklist	
☐ spelling	☐ subject-verb agreement
☐ capitalization	☐ indenting
☐ punctuation	☐ dates for each entry

2. Name two ways a journal is different from a regular story.

_____

_____

3. How does the author feel on April 19, 1849?

   a. happy
   b. bored
   c. excited
   d. tired

4. What is the main idea of the entry dated April 19, 1849?

   a. The scenery is changing from plains to mountains.
   b. The trip is taking longer than planned.
   c. Everything is the same day after day.
   d. The author is too tired to write in the journal each day.

5. Write another entry for this journal. Date it two months later: June 19, 1849. What do you think has happened? When you are finished, use the checklist to edit your work.

_____

_____

_____

The Great Oak Gang Mystery

A checklist is a tool to help you edit. In a story, indent for quotation marks whenever a new character speaks. Look for the beginning, middle, and end.

1. Use the following checklist to edit this story.

> ### Checklist
>
> ☐ spelling   ☐ story elements
> (beginning, middle, end)
> ☐ capitalization
> ☐ punctuation   ☐ indenting
> ☐ subject-verb agreement

The Great Oak Gang Mystery

"It's a mystery, said Azrina. "It just disappeaered." The whole Great Oak Gang talked at once. "How could it just disappear?" demanded scott. "Someone probably took it," shouted Nan. "yeah!" added Jerome. "One of those kids from park street coud have taken it."

Jerome explained why a kid from Park Street would take the ladder to there tree house. Scott explained why something couldnt just disappear. Nan tried not to listen to Scott or jerome. Finally, Azrina shouted for everyone's attention. "We can't climb into our treehouse. That doesn't meen this meeting can be out of order!" She looked at the great oak gang one by one. "Scott," she said, "we all know that the ladder couldn't just disappear That's just a saying. Jerome and Nan, there is no reson to suspect anyone from Park Street—at least, there's no reason yet. Let's work together to solve this mystry. now who was the last person to use the ladder?" "I suppose I was, said scott. "Two days ago," he added, "I ran out to the treehouse to escaape from my little sister for a while. Wen my mom called, I hurried back to the house. She was worried because of the storm. When I left, the ladder was hanging on the tree like always."

The members of the Great Oak Gang all agreed that Scott was the last to yuse the ladder.

The Great Oak Gang Mystery (cont.)

With the terrible storms yesterdy, none of them had gone to the tree house. "So mabe the storm blew it away," suggested azrina. No way," said Scott. "Those winds were strong, but so is the ladder. With the thick ropes, the whole thing was very heavy. I don't think the wind was strong enuf to blow the ladder away."

Again, the great oak gang agreed. The wind probably didn't blow their ladder away. Maybe the wind unhooked it from the tree Then Nan said she had familie clean up the yard. She picked up a lot of broken branches near the tree. Then she helped her dad and mom rack up a huge pile of leaves. Nan told the others that she didn't see the ladder while they where cleaning up the yard. "If it didn't blow away and you didn't see it while you cleaned up the yard, then where could it go?" asked Azrina. The Great Oak Gang was quite, until Jerome spoke up. "Nan, where was the huge pile of leafes?" he asked.

"All around the tree," she stated. Then she yelled, "All around our tree! I bet the ladder was picked up with the leaves!" Ten minutes later, after searching through bags of leaves, the Great Oak Gang had they're ladder back.

2. When does a new paragraph begin? Circle all of the correct answers.
   a. when someone different speaks
   b. when the author chooses
   c. when there is a pause in the story
   d. when the main idea changes
   e. whenever there is a transition word

3. What is the mystery in the story?

   _____

   _____

4. How is the mystery solved?

   _____

   _____

The Last Word

Editing poetry requires a special checklist. Editors must check all of the items to edit a poem well.

Read the poem. Answer the questions that follow.

The last word

Said the cat in the tree to the bird,	Sed the cat then, a littel bit louder,
"I don't now whether youve heard,	Step closer if you are a doubter."
But I'm getting thiner,	But the bird have a plan—
and I'm looking for dinner"	put thee cat in a pan
But the bird never herd a word.	and in minites had kitty cat chowder

1. Which of these checklists is best for editing this poem?
   a. Checklist A
   b. Checklist B

Checklist A
☐ spelling
☐ capitals in title
☐ capitals to begin each line
☐ punctuation at ends of lines
☐ quotation marks

Checklist B
☐ spelling
☐ capitals in title
☐ capitals to begin each line
☐ topic sentence and supporting details
☐ date in the heading

2. Why?

   _____

   _____

   _____

3. Using the correct checklist, edit this poem. Use proofreading marks to fix the mistakes. Some lines don't require end punctuation, but fix any lines that have wrong or missing end punctuation.

Name _____   Date _____

The Space Race

Editing poetry requires a special checklist. Editors must check all of the items to edit a poem well.

1. Read the poem. Use the checklist to help you edit the poem. Use proofreading marks to fix the mistakes. Some lines don't require end punctuation, but fix any lines that have wrong or missing end punctuation.

Checklist	
☐ spelling	☐ punctuation at ends of lines
☐ capitals in title	☐ commas after prepositional phrases
☐ capitals to begin each line	☐ extra or missing words

The space race

There is no species like human race.

Although they have a planet, they want space!

They bild up towers, tall and straight and round.

they launch them skyward—candles upsid down

In labs that orbit earth their time is a spent

On trying to invent things to invent.

They toil over evry last detail.

sometimes they win and othur times they fial.

Oh, silly humen race, do you beleive

that to love the earth you simply must leave?

You do not not nead more satellite TV!

by spending time outdoors, you might bee free!

2. What is the main difference between a story and a poem in terms of capital letters?

_____

_____

The River King

Editing poetry requires a special checklist. Editors must check all of the items to edit a poem well.

1. Read the poem. Use the checklist on page 91 to edit the poem. Use proofreading marks to fix the mistakes.

the River King

(1) A lovely maid
With <u>yellow</u> hair
danced and sang across a a field.

(2) A river rusched
Across her path.
The raging waters would not yield.

(3) Nowhere a bridge
to help her cross,
The maid was taken by her tears.

(4) She fell to her knees,
hands at her face.
The rivers rumble filled her ears.

(5) From in the reeds
Along the the bank
Awoke the dozing River King.

(6) He begged the maid
"Plaese do not <u>cry</u>.
I'd love to hear the song you sing."

(7) She wipped her eye,
then smoothed her gown
She poured her voice out into to song.

(8) The River King
Had never felt
A maiden voice flow out so strong.

(9) The Rivr King
reached for her hand
to lift the singing maiden high

(10) He brot her safe
Past river's rush,
Then wisht her well. "Sweet maid, good-bye."

The River King (cont.)

Checklist

☐ spelling   ☐ punctuation at ends of lines

☐ capitals in title   ☐ quotation marks

☐ capitals to begin each line   ☐ extra or missing words

---

2. Look at the items on the checklist. Which of these should be included on checklists for all types of writing? (Hint: Include stories, reports, poems, and letters.)

 a. capitals to begin each line, spelling, punctuation at the ends of lines
 b. quotation marks, capitals in title, spelling, capitals to begin each line
 c. spelling, quotation marks, extra or missing words
 d. capitals in title, capitals to begin each line, spelling

3. Which item on this checklist is found only on a checklist for poetry?

 a. spelling
 b. capitals in title
 c. extra or missing words
 d. capitals to begin each line

Word choice is very important in poetry. Two words are underlined in the poem. Choose a different word that means nearly the same as the underlined word. To choose the best word, find one that matches the language used in the poem.

4. In the first stanza, <u>yellow</u> could be replaced with—

 a. dark
 b. light
 c. red
 d. golden

5. In the sixth stanza, <u>cry</u> could be replaced with—

 a. bawl
 b. yell
 c. weep
 d. blubber

       91   0-7424-2754-4 *Proofreading & Editing*

Back to Basics

Different types of **punctuation** are the road signs of writing. They tell the reader when someone is speaking. They tell the reader when to slow down. They also tell the reader when a thought is complete. **Capital letters** also help readers identify different kinds of information.

Certain words or phrases must be capitalized. Edit the following sentences for capitalization.

1. on december 7, 1941, the japanese attacked pearl harbor.

2. our old house was in central city, kansas.

3. "could we please," carl asked his grandma, "have some ice cream?"

4. dr. shard asked us to come by his office on tuesday.

Choose the sentence that shows the correct capitalization.

5. a. That book's title is *Number the stars.*
    b. It was written by a very talented author named lois lowry.
    c. Dad said, "that book is fascinating."
    d. Mom gave me a copy of the book for my birthday, May 1.

6. a. The geese remind me of life in Canada.
    b. Shanti called Ahmal and said, "can you travel with my family in June?"
    c. Our neighbor, mr. Kaminski, is very kind.
    d. When I grow up, I want to write a book like the harry potter books.

Choose the sentence that shows the correct punctuation.

7. a. Our teacher moved here from Bangor, Maine on August 4 2002.
    b. "Please, think about it, said Mayor Hill.
    c. I wanted to buy Mom a present, said Eric, "but I don't have any money."
    d. The hot air balloon took us over 6,500 feet above Lake Elrod.

8. a. In 1849 people came from miles around to seek gold in the West.
    b. She is going to 54 Peacock Lane in New York, New York.
    c. Charlene cant find the golden necklace you bought in Dallas, Texas.
    d. Hurry, please, and join your father," called Mom.

Back to Basics (cont.)

Rewrite these sentences using the correct capitalization and punctuation.

9. after all of that we still didnt know how edward would get to johns game

   _____

   _____

10. do you want to go to the ball now asked cinderellas fairy godmother

   _____

   _____

   _____

11. Correct capitalization and punctuation are important in all types of writing. Edit this letter to correct both of these.

   november 22 2004

   dear aunt lola

   i cant wait to see you the summer is just too far away

   love

   farina

12. Circle all of the types of writing that you should edit for capitalization and punctuation.

   a. stories
   b. letters
   c. reports
   d. instructions
   e. lists

   f. homework
   g. explanations
   h. notes
   i. poems

13. In what types of writing should you edit for commas after the greeting and closing?

   a. stories
   b. letters
   c. reports
   d. instructions

14. Quotations are most likely to be found in what type of writing?

   a. letters
   b. instructions
   c. stories
   d. explanations

           0-7424-2754-4 *Proofreading & Editing*

Spell Well

A word that is spelled wrong can make something hard to read. Even worse, misspelled words can be confusing. Always edit your writing for correct spelling.

Choose the correct spelling.

1. a. tomorow
    b. tommorow
    c. tomorrow
    d. tommorro

2. a. because
    b. becuz
    c. becaus
    d. becuse

Choose the correct word to complete each sentence.

3. Kyle _____ want to play.

    a. dosen't
    b. doesnt
    c. dosn't
    d. doesn't

4. Shantal loves to go to the _____ .

    a. libary
    b. liberary
    c. libarary
    d. library

Choose the sentence with no spelling mistakes.

5. a. The pond ripled in the breeze.
    b. We broght our brand new fishing poles with us.
    c. The worms we caught maked excellent bait!
    d. We baited our hooks and cast our lines into the pond.

6. a. It wasnt long before my brother felt a tug.
    b. He slowly reeled the line in, pulling aginst the fish.
    c. The fish was strong and made him work hard!
    d. A few rainbow trout woud make a great dinner!

7. a. Mom showed us how to cleen fish.
    b. Dad taught us the right way to cook them.
    c. The whole familie sat down to a delicious meal.
    d. Today was my favorite fisching day ever!

8. Choose all of the types of writing that you should check for spelling.

    a. letters
    b. stories
    c. reports
    d. instructions
    e. lists

    f. homework
    g. notes
    h. explanations
    i. poetry

94   0-7424-2754-4 *Proofreading & Editing*

Can You Sea What I Mean?

Homophones are words that *sound* the same but are not spelled the same. They also have different meanings. Edit all writing for homophones.

Circle the correct word or words to complete these sentences.

1. My (grate, great)-grandfather was a mayor.

2. The (cent, scent, sent) of roasted turkey filled the kitchen.

3. Jeremiah (red, read) the (whole, hole) book in an (hour, our)!

4. It was so nice to (meet, meat, mete) the musician.

5. The (principal, principle) is the head of our school.

6. The man (rode, rowed, road) the boat slowly across the lake.

7. The streetlight (shown, shone) brightly over the 59th Street Bridge.

8. The letter began, "(Deer, Dear) Mr. President."

9. (Who's, Whose) backpack is this?

10. During our game, the baseball soared (through, threw) Mr. Nantucket's window.

11. (You're, Your) going (to, two, too) the concert, (write, right)?

12. Should we study at (your, you're) house or (there, their, they're) house?

Read the following story. Edit for homophone mistakes. Use proofreading marks to fix the mistakes.

13.   Your in the center of the soccer field, and the game is tide. Suddenly, Antoine takes the chance to steel the ball. He seas that this teem can pass the ball well. He does not give them a chance. He knows they're will be no piece until it's over. So, he kicks the ball wear they least expect it—write over there heads! He scores! With this win, he mite move out of the miner leagues.

14. In what types of writing should you edit for homophones? List at least five types.

_____   _____

_____   _____

_____

◆◆◆

Farm Life

In all writing, the subject and verb must agree in number. Some verbs follow a pattern. Others do not follow a pattern. They must be memorized.

◆◆◆

Read these sentences. Choose the sentence in which the subject and verb agree.

1. a. The daffodils is all blooming on the hillside.
   b. A gentle rain wash the drowsiness from the waking earth.
   c. Seedlings wake from their long sleep.

2. a. My mother worries that her garden will not grow.
   b. Dad say that this autumn we should have a good harvest.
   c. Along the riverbank, my brothers hunts for frogs.

3. a. The plow and the oxen stands ready to plant another crop.
   b. Our coop is full of squawking chickens and crowing roosters.
   c. In the pigpen, hogs searches for their morning food.

4. a. Before the winter came, we harvested our crops.
   b. We'll plants beans next year.
   c. Our crops fills four wagons.

Read each sentence. Circle the form of the verb that agrees with the subject.

5. In the morning, we (has, have) to feed the horses, chickens, and hogs.

6. Dad (leave, leaves) after breakfast and (work, works) in the fields all day.

7. All of the household chores (are, is) finished by noon.

8. Each evening, my brother (brush, brushes) down the horse.

Use proofreading marks to fix the following sentences.

9. By the Fourth of July, Dad know if the crops will turn out well.

10. All last winter, we enjoys Mother's canned tomatoes.

11. The horses pulls the wagons, but the oxen pull the plow.

12. I loves the farm.

Secret to Success

Using the same type of sentence over and over bores the reader. Edit all writing to vary the sentences. As always, use correct spelling, capitalization, and punctuation.

Combine these short, boring sentences to create complex or compound sentences.

1. Markita ran to the motorcycle. Travis ran to the motorcycle. Markita started the motorcyle. Travis jumped on the motorcycle.

_____

_____

A sentence must be a complete thought. Finish the following thought to make a complete sentence.

2. When they finally reached the train, _____

_____

Sometimes a writer combines sentences that are not connected in any way. Rewrite these sentences correctly by breaking them into sentences that make sense.

3. Travis hopped in the car and drove away and when he got to the cave he parked the car inside and got out of the car.

_____

_____

Using a prepositional phrase at the beginning of a sentence is a good way to vary the type of sentence. Rearrange these sentences to put a prepositional phrase at the beginning.

4. The two spies fled the city under cover of night.

_____

_____

5. Travis made sure he stated the facts correctly in preparing his report.

_____

_____

Anchor Your Ideas

A topic sentence tells the main idea in a paragraph. Supporting sentences explain more about the main idea.

Circle the letter of the sentence that does not support the main idea.

1. Huge container ships carry goods around the world.

    a. Most large ports can handle container ships.
    b. When I visited Los Angeles, I saw a huge ship.
    c. Container ships use all of the major trade routes.

2. The containers are used as truck bodies and train cars.

    a. Each container is the same size and shape, but there are different colors.
    b. A container can be set on a flat truck or train bed.
    c. The ships are so large they can carry 1600 containers.

3. These ships make loading and unloading easy.

    a. The containers are stacked on the ship's deck.
    b. A large crane can unload one container at a time.
    c. Containers hold food, cars, or other cargo.

The topic sentence tells the main idea of a paragraph. Choose the best topic sentence for this paragraph.

4. _____ Goods used to be shipped by cargo ships. Cargo ships cost more to load and unload. Container ships have made it easy to take goods inland. The containers can be moved from the ship to a truck or a train. Also, a cargo ship could not carry as much. Container ships carry more goods to more countries.

    a. The containers can be used as truck bodies.
    b. Container ships do not sink as often as cargo ships.
    c. Cargo ships are rarely used to take goods inland.
    d. Container ships are better than cargo ships.

5. Circle the types of writing that you would edit for topic sentences and supporting details.

    a. poetry
    b. explanations
    c. stories
    d. reports
    e. lists
    f. letters

◆◇◆◇◆◇◆◇◆◇◆◇◆◇◆◇◆◇◆◇◆◇◆◇◆◇◆◇◆◇◆◇◆◇◆◇◆◇◆

Get the Point?

A paragraph is a group of sentences that tells the reader about one main idea. Beginning a new paragraph tells the reader that a new idea is coming. You should edit for correct paragraphs in all forms of writing. Start a new paragraph when the main idea changes, when a new character speaks, or when a speaking character changes the main idea.

◆◇◆◇◆◇◆◇◆◇◆◇◆◇◆◇◆◇◆◇◆◇◆◇◆◇◆◇◆◇◆◇◆◇◆◇◆◇◆

1. Read the following passage. Use the proofreading mark ¶ to show where two more paragraphs should begin.

    The swamp began to fill up with night and the noise of insects. The high chirp of crickets and the fluttering wings of moths blended in the darkness. "Do you think the crocs will stay away now?" asked Kiki Anne. "I'm too afraid to go to sleep knowing they are out there. What if they see the fire?" Pedro answered quickly, "You don't have to worry. I'm going to stay awake just to make sure we don't get a visit." He tried not to look tired.

2. Read the following passage from an article about bread making. Use editing marks to show where two additional paragraphs should begin.

    Many new bakers use too much flour when they knead the bread. Kneading is when the baker folds and presses the bread to create pockets of air. Using a lot of flour makes kneading easier, but it also makes the bread heavy. Another  mistake is to work the bread too hard. Kneading bread too long can make it tough. A good bread maker knows when to let the dough rest and for how long. The last trick new bakers need to know is how to make the crust just right. Baking a crunchy crust is different from baking a chewy crust. Spraying water on the crust as it bakes makes it chewier. Melted butter makes a crust crunchier.

                   0-7424-2754-4 *Proofreading & Editing*

The Key Word

Every piece of writing is different. A letter to a friend uses different words than a letter to a teacher. The editor must make sure that the words match the purpose and the audience.

Read the purpose and choose the best topic sentence.

1. **Purpose:** report to the class on whales
   a. Whales are a species of mammal that lives in the oceans.
   b. Whales are the coolest sea creatures because they are so huge.
   c. I am going to tell you all about whales.

2. **Purpose:** a story about a shipwreck
   a. The *Merlin*, a small clipper, left port at 2:37 P.M. and headed northeast.
   b. This is an awesome story about the building of the *Merlin*.
   c. When it left port, the *Merlin* set sail just like any other day.

3. Choose the type of closing used in a letter to your grandmother.
   a. Sincerely,
   b. Best regards,
   c. Love,

4. Choose the type of closing used in a letter to the mayor.
   a. Yours truly,
   b. Your friend,
   c. Hugs and kisses,

5. Which choice uses the right words for a lemonade recipe?
   a. Don't use unripe lemons. They are gross.
   b. Choose four or five medium-sized lemons.
   c. The lemon juice mixes with the water and sugar to make a solution.

Rewrite this sentence for each type of writing below. Remember to use appropriate words.

Sentence: The street is too busy to cross.

6. a letter to a friend _____

   _____

7. a letter to the mayor _____

   _____

Name _____   Date _____

Tell Me Why

Before writing, an author must know the reason for the piece and who will read it. The editor must also know the purpose and the audience.

Read the audience and purpose. Then choose the best topic to match.

1. **Audience:** a student from France
   Purpose: tell about life in the United States

   a. the American Revolution
   b. my trip to France
   c. a typical U.S. school day

2. **Audience:** a doctor
   Purpose: tell how your brother got hurt

   a. when my brother fell
   b. how to play tree tag
   c. the time I broke my arm

3. **Audience:** a race car driver
   Purpose: why a seat belt is important

   a. how fast race cars go
   b. when my dad was in an accident
   c. why I want to drive cars when I grow up

Read these titles and pick the best audience for each.

4. ____   "Why Students Don't Like Homework"   a. teachers

5. ____   "How to Write in a Different Language"   b. a mail carrier

6. ____   "My Father Directs a Singing Group"   c. a hockey team

7. ____   "Why First Grade Is Fantastic!"   d. a farmer

8. ____   "When I Worked in the Fields"   e. a choir

9. ____   "The Day I Scored Three Goals"   f. a Spanish writer

10. ____   "How Letters Are Sorted"   g. a kindergarten class

Not-So-Dandy Handy-Dandy

When you edit, you can make your own checklist for each type of writing.

Make your own checklist to edit the letter. Be sure to include the punctuation that follows the greeting and closing. Edit the letter using your checklist and the proofreading marks you have learned.

Checklist

- ☐ _____
- ☐ _____
- ☐ _____
- ☐ _____
- ☐ _____

Shandra L. Itzak

651 Rustling pines Rd

Manchester new hampshire 00564

february 10 2006

To Whom It May Concern:

Last week, I boght a bottle of your Handy-Dandy Hair Softener Last night I tried it. It did not make my hair soft and shinny after the first use. Instead, it turned my hair purple

Not only do I wants my money back but I also neeed to know what to do about my hair. I has already washed it for times, but the purple color will *not* go away I am wearing a cap to hide it but i can't wear the cap forever. My littel brother and his friends think this is is hilarious, but I don't!

Please call me wit a solution to this problem an give me back my money. I will *never* by products from your company again

You're angry customer

Shandra L. Itzak

Think about it! How does Shandra feel? Does this help you understand some of the end marks in this letter?

A Special Grandfather

When you make a checklist for editing a letter, be sure to look for mistakes that happen only in letters.

Make your own checklist to edit the letter. Edit the letter using your checklist and the proofreading marks you have learned.

Checklist

☐ _____

☐ _____

☐ _____

☐ _____

☐ _____

☐ _____

"Mom? I found this letter in that old box in the attic. Is this our painting in the living room? And is 'Sweet Patooties' you?" asked the red-haired child.

"Yes, Honey," said Mom. "That's the letter I wrote to my grandfather many years ago when he painted that picture for me. What a special gift that was!"

February 14 1977

Dear Grandpa dexter,

What a beautiful oil painting you sent I can't beleive how it real it looks—just like Dad and me. Has you always ben able to paint that well? mom helped me choose an oak fraem for the painting. It looks great The Colors you chose matchd the lake and the sunset exactly! Dad saed that the talent to create art like this is a a true gift. I agree. It was so nice of you to shair this gift with us.

yesterday, Dad and I hung the painting over the couch in the living room. It will staey on the wall forever. It will stay in our hearts, two.

Thank you vary much, Grandpa.

With all my love

Sweet Patooties

Name _____   Date _____

The Man and the Cat

Writers give information in reports. Reports must be clear and correct. The editor needs to check the facts in a report. The facts must match the facts from the source.

Read the following report about Dr. Seuss. Then follow the instructions on page 105.

The man and the cat

On march 2 1904, a baby boy were born. His name was Theodor Seuss geisel. He grew up in Springfield Massachusetts. When he was old enough, he went to a college called Dartmouth. He studied English writers and there books. After graduating from Dartmouth in 1925, he moved to England. He went to school at Oxford but he never Finnish his classes there. Instead, in 1927, he married Helen Palmer, a girl he met at school. They moves back to the united states. Theodore sold cartoons that he drew He sold them to magazines. Later, theodor worked on his first book. he tried to sell it to a book company. The book company didnt want it. The company told him his book was two different. Theodore did not give up. He took his book to one company after another. Twenty-six companies told him they didn't not like his book. The twenty-seventh company buyed it! His first book, *And to Think That I Saw It on Mulberry Stret*, sold in 1937. When the company asket him what name he wanted on his book, he told them "Dr Seuss."

After his first book, Dr. Seuss wrote 43 mor. He wrote *The Cat in the Hat* in 1975. It was a book that students could enjoy whiel they were learning to read. Dr. Seuss became vary popular. His books thrilled children and parents

In 1959, a man made a bet with Dr. Seuss. He bet Dr Seuss that he could not write a whole book using olny 50 different words. In 1960, Dr Seuss winned that bet! He wrote *Green Eggs and Ham.*

Dr. Seuss lived to be 87 years old. He won many awards for his wonderful work. He changes the way writers write for children

         0-7424-2754-4 *Proofreading & Editing*

Name _____ Date _____

The Man and the Cat (cont.)

Read this source for the report on page 104.

Source: Timeline of Dr. Seuss's Life

1904	1925	1927	1937	1939–1945	1957	1984	1991
Born in Springfield	Graduated from Dartmouth	Married Helen Palmer	Published his first book, *And to Think That I Saw It on Mulberry Street*	Wrote training movies for the U.S. Army	Published *The Cat in the Hat*	Won a Pulitzer Prize	Died

1. Create a checklist of the items you need to check in a report. Remember to edit for clear and correct details.

Checklist

☐ _____

☐ _____

☐ _____

☐ _____

☐ _____

☐ _____

2. What facts from the timeline were not used?

_____

_____

3. Why do you think the author did not use these facts?

_____

_____

_____

4. Which fact from the report does not match the timeline?
   a. married Helen Palmer in 1927
   b. born in Springfield in 1904
   c. published *The Cat in the Hat* in 1975
   d. graduated from Dartmouth in 1925

Stonehenge

Writers give information in reports. Reports must be clear and correct. The editor must check the facts in a report. The facts must match the facts from the source. A statement in quotation marks must be exactly as it is in the source.

Read the report on Stonehenge. Then read the source material on page 107. Follow the instructions.

Stonehenge

In southwestern England lives a mystrey. There is an ancient ring of huge stones. Very little is knowed about this place called Stonehenge. Will anyone ever unlock its secrets, or are they lost in the past forever Peggy brown has studied this mystery her whole life. "I grew up near Stonehenge, she says. "Some days after school, I would go there sit on the stones, and just imagine. I tried to picture the people who builded it." She has done more than imagine. Peggy Brown has written three books on Stonehenge. There are some facts we know about when Stonehenge was built. as early as 2000 B.C., people had already dug the outer ditch and bank of dirt. People were still finished parts of Stonehenge in 1500 B.C. It went through many changes. "I really wonder if the people who finished it knew what the people who starts it wanted, says Peggy Brown. She doesn't not think so. There were to many changes along the way.

There are many theories about how Stonehenge was built. Experts have make models of how the builders stood and stacked the rocks Experts have figurd out how the huge stones could be moved so far. Peggy Brown says, "We may already understand how they built Stonehenge." The most difficult question to anser is *why*? Why was Stonehenge built, rebuilt, and changed Some say it was a kind of temple. others say it was a calendar. The qestion why is the door to all of the answers. sadly, no one has the key.

Stonehenge (cont.)

Source 1: A passage from Peggy Brown's newest book, *Leave No Stone Unturned*

"I grew up near Stonehenge. I thought about it a lot. It was as if it called out to me. Some days after school, I'd go there, sit on the stones, and just imagine. I tried to picture the people who built it. I tried to imagine why they built it and how they used it. It took so long to build, and there were so many changes along the way. I really wonder if the people who finished it knew what the people who started it wanted."

Source 2: The Building Phases of Stonehenge

Date	Building Phase
3000 B.C.	Stonehenge begins. A large, round ditch and bank of dirt are made. Fifty-six small holes are dug in a ring inside the larger bank.
2100 B.C.	The Bluestones are placed. Huge stones from 240 miles away stand in shallow holes to make two circles—one inside the other.
2000 B.C.	The Sarsen stones are added. These stones sit in holes. Then more stones are laid across the tops of the standing stones. They are set up in the shape of a horseshoe.
1500 B.C.	Bluestones are moved to a ring inside the Sarsen stone circle.
1100 B.C.	The Avenue is lengthened. A dirt road, or avenue, stretches from Stonehenge for over half a mile.

1. What facts in the report must be changed to match the information in the source?

   _____

   _____

2. Edit the report on page 106 after you make a checklist to remind you of the items you need to check. Remember to edit for clear and correct details. Also, be sure the facts from your sources match the facts in the report.

   Checklist

   ☐ _____
   ☐ _____
   ☐ _____
   ☐ _____
   ☐ _____
   ☐ _____
   ☐ _____

Name   Date

Olaf's Adventure

To help you edit a **story,** your checklist should remind you to look for the elements of a story—setting, characters, beginning, middle, and end. Do the characters speak? Is the story complete? Do paragraph breaks make sense?

Read the story. Then follow the instructions on page 109.

Olaf peered through the tinted glass of his helmet. He surched for the shape he thought he had seen. He squinted and held his gloved hand up to block the dazzling light of the sun. He scanned the rocks and craters 30 meeters ahead. He saw nothing

Olafs helmet radio buzzed to life. "Base-Com 6 to Scout 22. Report! do you copy?"

"Twenty-two" said olaf. I'm checking into a sighting near the barracks. I have nothing to report yet but I'm going to . . ." Olaf stoppet. He saw one of the stones trembling. He whispered harshly, "Stand by!" Olaf raised his right hand to block the sunliht. He slowly circled to his right. He watching the stone. He krept toward it.

With the stone just a few meters away, Olaf's blood froze. His breathing grew heavy. He had to chewse which side of the stone to explore first. Olaf decided to keep to the sunny side of the rock. He walked sidways around the rock, and he looked for a stone in case he would have to throw one. Just as his eyes found the stone, a sudden flash of gray bolted passed him. olaf let out a shriek. Then he laffed. He clicked on his radeo again. "Scout 22 to Base-Com 6, come in. No sighting near the barracks. It was just a nite worm. It must have been caught by the sunrise. It scared me when it dashed off, but we're are both fine now. Olaf turned off the radio and strolled back to baase.

       0-7424-2754-4 *Proofreading & Editing*

Name _____   Date _____

Olaf's Adventure (cont.)

Circle the correct answer to each question about the story elements in "Olaf's Adventure" on page 108.

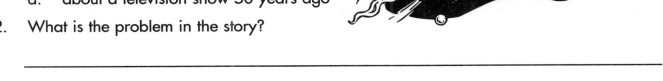

1. What is the setting in the story?
   a. on Earth 100 years ago
   b. on another planet at daybreak
   c. in a war zone in the future
   d. about a television show 50 years ago

2. What is the problem in the story?

   _____

   _____

3. The **climax** of a story leads to the solution of the problem. It is the highest point of excitement. It occurs right before the end. What sentence tells the climax of the story?
   a. Olaf turned off the radio and strolled back to base.
   b. Olaf let out a shriek.
   c. "It scared me when it dashed off, but we're both fine now."
   d. He saw one of the stones trembling.

4. What is the solution to the main character's problem?

   _____

   _____

5. Make your own checklist to edit this story. Then use the checklist to edit the story for all errors. Do the characters speak? Is the story complete? Are the paragraph breaks correct?

Checklist
☐ _____
☐ _____
☐ _____
☐ _____
☐ _____
☐ _____
☐ _____

       0-7424-2754-4 *Proofreading & Editing*

A Bittersweet Day

To help you edit a story, your checklist should remind you to look for the elements of a story—a beginning, a middle, and an end. Do the characters speak? Is the story complete? Do paragraph breaks make sense?

Read the story. Then follow the instructions on page 111.

Mrs Whitney and I dusted the porcelain figures she had collected all of her life. She was from dresden germany. the figures had all been were made there. They were sew beautiful. I wished hard I could have one of my very own

Suttenly, it happend again. The delicate figure slipped threw her fingers. it shattered on the flour. "Oh, dear!" said Mrs. whitney. she stoooped to pick up the pieces. I ran to help her.

"Mrs. Whitney has been having troubles holding on to things lately, Mom," I remarked as Mom and I did the dishes together that night.

"Mrs. Whitney is getting olderer, Alex. That's all, said Mom. "But Mom, she dropped anuther figurine. Her hands are shaking really hard."

Mom sighed. Maybe it's time to let her son know about this"

The next day, Mom called Mrs. Whitneys son. He lives about 60 miles away. On sunday, he stopped by our house. "Alex, he said, "you were right. My mother needs some help. She isn't abel to do evreything she used to do. I didn't no how much you was helping her. Mom said that if you hadn't not helped her, she could not have gotten through each day. I want to thank you!"

"What will you do now" asked Mom.

"Mother will be moving in with me so I can help her. Alex, Mother and I would like you to come over tomorow afternoon. She wants you to pick out your favrite figurine. She'd like you to have it to remember her." Tomorrow will be strange day, I thought. I will finlly have my very own Dresden figurine. But I must say good-bye to my best friend. Mom says that days like this are called *bittersweet.* I think I know wat she means

Name _____   Date _____

A Bittersweet Day (cont.)

1. Create your own checklist. Use it to edit the story. Use proofreading marks to fix the mistakes.

Checklist

☐ _____

☐ _____

☐ _____

☐ _____

☐ _____

☐ _____

☐ _____

2. What is the problem in the story?

   a. The main character wants her own Dresden figurine.
   b. Mrs. Whitney is having trouble holding on to things.
   c. Mrs. Whitney's son will not help her.
   d. Mom doesn't want Alex to help Mrs. Whitney.

3. The main character says that she knows what *bittersweet* means. Based on the story, what does it mean? (Hint: Break the word into two words you know.)

_____

_____

_____

_____

Make It Shine! On another sheet of paper, write a story about an event that was bittersweet for you. Use the checklist you created for this story to edit your work.

Make It Even Better!

Revising is not the same as editing. When you edit, you find and fix mistakes in the writing. When you **revise,** you rewrite to make the writing better. A few ways to revise are to choose better words, to add details, and to combine sentences.

Revising begins with each sentence. Here are ways to make your sentences better:

Use vivid verbs and words that are more specific.

Example: She <u>went</u> <u>home</u>.

               She <u>zoomed</u> <u>to her adobe home at the edge of the cliff</u>.

Combine sentences and add more details.

Example: Cory <u>came over to my house</u>. I <u>found out I was going to Hawaii</u>.

               Just <u>after I found out that my family was going to Hawaii</u>, Cory <u>came over to my house to tell me that his family was going, too!</u>

Revise these four sentences. Use both of the strategies listed above.

1. Abdul won the game.

    _____

    _____

2. She went to the fair. She rode the rides there.

    _____

    _____

3. The stuff was all wet.

    _____

    _____

4. The show was good. We loved it!

    _____

    _____

Name ·   Date

Make It Your Best!

All paragraphs can be made better. To revise a paragraph, make sure that all of the thoughts are about the same main idea. Vary the sentences in type and length. Revise words that repeat by finding synonyms. Shorten ideas that are too long or complicated.

Read these paragraphs. Then revise them to make them fantastic!

1.   Dawn crept across the sky. Dawn scared away the night. Dawn reached orange fingers into the darkness. Dawn brought light to the forests and fields. Bats began their sleep. Birds began their song. Shadows shrank and disappeared. Shadows fled the forest.

_____

_____

_____

_____

_____

_____

2.   Before Columbus came to America, there was no corn in Europe. The Native Americans grew corn. When the Pilgrims came from Europe, they did not know what corn was. Native Americans showed the Pilgrims how to grow corn. When a ship sailed to Europe, it carried corn back to Europe. Before that, there was no corn in Europe.

_____

_____

_____

_____

_____

_____

_____

                   0-7424-2754-4 *Proofreading & Editing*

Cadillac Lake

When you revise a letter, think about the reader. Focus on what the author is trying to say. Is it clear? Are these the best words to use?

Read the following letter. Edit the letter for spelling and punctuation.

August 6, 2005

Dear Mom and Dad,

    Thanks so much for letting me visit Grandma and Grandpa in Michigan. (⇨) We have been hiking around. We go around Cadillac Lake every morning and every evening and sometimes in the afternoon. Grandpa likes to make his birdcall make the bird noise to see what birds he can get to listen to his bird call and answer him with their birdcalls back to him. Grandma uses the blackberries from around here to make jelly. It is the jelly that we like. We like it so much! When you come to pick me up, we can make that delicious jelly that we like so much. We can do that together. (⇨) See you next Thursday!

                Love,

                Jack

Revise the letter to make it better. Rewrite only the part of the letter between (⇨) marks. When you finish, make a checklist and edit any mistakes in your revision.

_____

_____

_____

_____

_____

_____

_____

_____

Homemade Ice Cream

When revising instructions, review each step. Make each step clear and complete. Check to see that the steps are in the correct order. Include enough detail to leave no questions in the reader's mind.

Read the instructions.

Homemade Ice Cream

1. To make the ice cream, you need a small plastic zipping freezer bag.
2. In the smaller bag, place 1 cup of whole milk, $\frac{1}{4}$ teaspoon of vanilla flavoring, and 4 tablespoons of powdered sugar. Zip tightly.
3. Unzip the larger bag and discard the ice and salt. Remove and dry the smaller bag. Unzip to enjoy your own homemade ice cream!
4. Add some ice and rock salt to the larger bag.
5. Squeeze the air out of the larger bag and seal it well. Shake the bag for about five minutes.

Rewrite the instructions here. Make them clear and easy to understand. When you finish revising, edit your work.

_____

_____

_____

_____

_____

_____

_____

_____

_____

_____

_____

Name _____   Date _____

Waste Not, Want Not

When you revise a report, make sure the facts are clear. Use your sentence revision skills to make the writing better. Be sure to remove any facts that are not needed for the report.

Read the following report. Then follow the numbered instructions.

Waste Not, Want Not

Every year, Americans throw away more and more garbage. Every year, more than 200 million tons of trash go to landfills. Every year, trash pollutes land, air, rivers, and lakes. Trash is really gross and often smells bad. This pollution is bad enough, but the story gets worse. Next year, America will produce more trash. What if there were a way to reuse last year's trash and reduce this year's trash? There is! Recycling may be the best way to save our planet from the trash.

1. One sentence does not support the main idea of this paragraph. Use the proofreading mark to delete it.

2. The first three sentences of this report sound the same. On the lines below, revise them to keep the reader's interest.

_____

_____

_____

_____

_____

_____

_____

_____

_____

_____

Waste Not, Want Not (cont.)

Read the next section of the report. Then follow the numbered instructions.

The table below shows a few types of waste. It shows aluminum. It shows steel. It shows plastic. It shows glass. It shows the amounts of each type of waste. It shows the recycled percent. It shows that plastic has the lowest percent. It shows that steel has the highest percent. This table shows how much America recycles.

Type of Waste	Amount	Percent Recycled
Aluminum	100 billion cans	65%
Steel	37 billion cans	68%
Plastic	38 billion pounds	4.7%
Glass	27.3 billion pounds	33%

This paragraph of the report does not help a reader understand the information given in the table.

3. To revise the paragraph, circle two or three facts that you think best support the theme of recycling instead of throwing away.

4. Rewrite the paragraph. Use the facts that you circled to show the reader that there is too much trash and not enough recycling.

_____

_____

_____

_____

_____

Read the next section of the report. Then follow the numbered instructions.

The United States recycles 45 million tons of trash each year. That means 45 million tons of trash do not go into a landfill. It also means that new goods can come from recycled wastes. Americans can learn to reuse more. Then maybe the planet will not be trashed.

5. The last sentence of this paragraph does not use language that's right for a report. Rewrite the last sentence to fit the theme of the report.

_____

_____

     117   0-7424-2754-4 *Proofreading & Editing*

A Very Cold Journey

When revising a story, make sure the writing keeps the reader's interest. Vary the types of sentences used in the story. Also, change the length of the sentences so they are not all the same.

Read the following short story. Then follow the numbered instructions.

Ice was everywhere. Ice surrounded our small ship. Ice was in front and behind. Ice was to port and starboard. Ice was all we could see far off to the horizon. Ice made creaking noises. Ice made groaning noises. Ice slowly crushed our ship.

1. Combine the short sentences into longer, more interesting sentences. Vary the sentences so they do not all start the same way.

_____

_____

_____

Read the next section of the story. Then follow the numbered instructions.

The whole crew jumped out of the ship. One day, it finally happened. The ice burst through the hull of our ship. Freezing water poured in. The ship started to sink. We grabbed some food. We grabbed some blankets and gear. The whole crew stood on the ice and watched as our ship nodded under the water. Later, the ice sealed the hole.

2. Revise this paragraph to be clear and short. Make sure the sentences are in the right order. Also, take out sentences that repeat the same idea.

_____

_____

_____

_____

_____

_____

A Very Cold Journey (cont.)

Read the next section of the story. Then follow the numbered instructions.

Night's cold fingers reached under our blankets. We couldn't stay warm. We built small fires from pieces of the ship. The fire gave us some warmth. The whole crew was worried. We knew the ice would not melt. We knew there would be no rescue. The cold was everywhere. Even when we built small fires, the warmth lasted only a short time. The cold air was like a knife. The cold morning was cruel. We didn't know how long we would last. We were worried. When would the rescue ships come?

3. This paragraph repeats many ideas. Delete any extra information. Revise the paragraph to be clear and short.

_____

_____

_____

_____

_____

Read the conclusion of the story. Then follow the numbered instructions.

Our only hope was to rescue ourselves. We built small sleds from the ship's planks. We loaded our gear. We walked across the ice. We didn't know which way to go. We had to climb over rocks. We had to run across broken ice bridges. We had to swim across small channels. We lost one sled. We lost all of the gear. Finally, we came to land. We still were not safe. We had to find shelter. We had to find food. We found a small village. The villagers took care of us. They saved us. We lived.

4. In this paragraph, many of the sentences begin the same way. Revise the paragraph to be more interesting. Vary the type and length of the sentences.

_____

_____

_____

_____

_____

Answer Key

Mark It Right
- Pages 4–5
1. For our vacation, Mom is taking us to England!
2. I want to see the clock called Big Ben.
3. After we see London, we are going to Cambridge.
4. Mom says that travel helps people learn.
5. Look! There's the Tower of London!
6. Paragraph starts with: This summer, Mom and I are flying to London.
7. Mom and I will eat a special dish called fish and chips.
8. At the end of the trip, we will stop to see my grandparents before coming home.

At the End
- Page 6
1. Tiana had an ancestor who escaped from the South.
2. Did you learn about Harriet Tubman?
3. I want to visit an Underground Railroad station.
4. What? There is one in our town?
5. That's exciting news!
6. On Friday, our class went on a field trip. We were so excited! We went to see an old house in our town. It used to be a hiding place for people. It was a station on the Underground Railroad. "Is there a secret room here?" we asked. There was! It was behind a wall in the cellar. The door had shelves on the outside. When it was closed, it looked just like part of the wall.
7. Answers will vary.

Journal Journeys
- Page 7
1. ?
2. . or !
3. .
4. .
5. .
6. !
7. ?
8. ?
9.
10. When will you write in your journal?
11. I have my journal from third grade.
12. Write faster!
13. Can I read what you wrote?

More Journal Journeys
- Page 8
1. Along with helping you remember things, journals help you learn to write better.
2. For example, say you wanted to write about a funny experience you had at school.
3. You can look it up in your journal, and you can read about it.
4. My journal is about my life in Denver, Colorado.
5. I have my second-grade journals, and I have a journal from third grade.
6. Journals make writing fun!
7. It was my brother who took my journal.
8. My teacher gave me a new blank book, and I used it to start a journal.
9. Did you see the new book about keeping a journal?

Exploring Punctuation
- Page 9
1. d
2. b
3. a
4. b
5. Along with his son, Hudson was set adrift in a boat.
6. We'll never know what happened to them.
7. You can drive to Hudson Bay through Ontario, Canada.

Columbus
- Page 10
1. "I think Columbus was very brave," said Jonathan.
2. "When he set sail, he didn't know if he would ever reach land again," Tiana said. "I bet his crew was scared."
3. "Their journey must have been hard," Ms. Rodriguez added. "But the crew must have trusted Columbus."
4. "I would have wanted to go home!" said Yong.
5. "If they had gone home," said Maria, "then we wouldn't be here today!"
6. "Good point, Maria!" said Ms. Rodriguez.
7. "What will we do," asked Tiana, "at our party?"
8. Ms. Rodriguez said, "We are going to play a game about explorers."

A Letter from Steven
- Page 11
Punctuation in the letter includes errors in end marks and interior marks; missing quotation marks in Grandpa's words; and commas missing in the date, opening, and closing.

One Summer Morning
- Page 12
1. Punctuation in the story includes errors in end marks and interior marks, missing quotation marks in the first and second paragraphs, and commas missing from a series at the end of the third paragraph.
2. Answers will vary.

Inspiring Leaders
- Page 13
1. c
2. a
3. c
4. Red Cloud helped win land for the Lakota tribe.
5. Chief Joseph was a famous nineteenth-century leader.
6. Today, Wilma Mankiller lives in Oklahoma.
7. Mankiller is still an important leader of the Cherokee people.

Native-American Places
- Page 14
1. b
2. c
3. a
4. Long before Europeans came to America, many different tribes settled the land. One famous tribe was the Iroquois. The Iroquois lived in the mountains of New York and Pennsylvania. The Ojibwa lived in Michigan and in other places around the Great Lakes. The Lakota tribe was strong and powerful. They lived on the prairie in North Dakota and South Dakota. In Idaho, the Nez Percé was a peaceful tribe of traders and horse trainers.

Answer Key

Janna's Schedule
• Page 15
1. c
2. b
3. b
4. Do you think Janna can <u>s</u>leep over on <u>F</u>riday or <u>S</u>aturday?
5. Janna is going to a concert on <u>F</u>riday, April 4.
6. <u>F</u>riday's concert tickets are for <u>J</u>anna's birthday.
7. Janna goes to <u>s</u>wimming lessons during <u>J</u>uly and August.
8. Her favorite day of the week is <u>M</u>onday.
9. Janna is moving to a new house next <u>S</u>aturday.
10. She will start school on <u>W</u>ednesday, September 4.

All About Bears
• Page 16
1. <u>A</u> bear can eat 35 pounds of fish at a time.
2. <u>S</u>ome bears weigh almost 2,000 pounds.
3. The stuffed teddy bear was named after <u>P</u>resident <u>T</u>heodore <u>R</u>oosevelt.
4. <u>M</u>ost bear cubs are born in November.
5. <u>B</u>ears are found in many states.
6. The <u>N</u>orth American grizzly bear is rare in the United <u>S</u>tates.
7. There is a famous short story called "<u>T</u>he <u>B</u>ear."
8. In Asia, bears are trained to dance.
9. Panda bears from <u>C</u>hina are not really bears.
10. Brown bears are found in <u>A</u>sia, <u>E</u>urope, and <u>N</u>orth <u>A</u>merica.
11. Answers will vary.

An American Hero
• Page 17
1. The report should be edited for name and place capitalization, for misplaced capital letters on common nouns, for the capitalization of *Supreme Court*, and for the capitalization of *African-American*.
2. a
3. a
4. c
5. a

Fashion Sense
• Page 18
1. c
2. a
3. d
4. b
5. b
6. Everyone loves to <u>wear</u> blue <u>jeans</u>.
7. I have a new pair of <u>running</u> shoes.

Sounds the Same!
• Page 19
1. horse
2. week
3. to, too
4. hare
5. plane
6. sea
7. That jacket was <u>cheap</u>.
8. I am <u>too</u> tired to go to the movies.

9. Did you <u>buy</u> a <u>pair</u> of pants?
10. It was a dark and stormy <u>night</u>.

Another Word?
• Page 20
1. c
2. b
3. c
4. a
5. c
6.–7. Answers will vary. Examples: cooling, long, slow, or unhurried.

Velvet's Class
• Page 21
1. b
2. a
3. b
4. a
5. a
6. Answers will vary.

Don't Do It!
• Page 22
1. c
2. c
3. b
4. a
5. c.
6. I didn't have <u>any</u> money.
7. I <u>can</u> hardly wait to go.
8. I didn't know <u>anybody</u> there.

Many Meanings
• Page 23
1. d
2. d
3. c
4. d
5. a
6. c
7. d

Many Monsters
• Pages 24–25
1. like
2. look
3. looks
4. is
5. use
6. are
7. are
8. My sister lov<u>es</u> to go to the movies.
9. We <u>sit</u> up in the balcony.
10. My mom <u>buys</u> us popcorn.
11. b
12. a
13. c
14. There <u>is</u> a spider in my bed!
15. I scream <u>when</u> I see it.

Answer Key

16. My mom run<u>s</u> into the room.
17. I see the spider as it run<u>s</u> across the room.
18. Mom pick<u>s</u> it up on a newspaper and takes it outside.
19. I make my bed again and tuck<u> </u>in the sheets tightly.
20. If another spider show<u>s</u><u> </u>up, it won't be able to get in!

Awful Ellen
• Pages 26–27
1. My cousin Ellen <u>is</u> just awful!
2. Whenever she comes to our house, someone <u>gets</u> into trouble.
3. She always talk<u>s</u> us into doing something we're not supposed to do.
4. She won't let anybody say <u>anything</u> about it, either.
5. One time, Ellen <u>told</u> everybody to skip balls against Mrs. White's house.
6. My brother <u>threw</u> the ball against a window.
7. Nobody else did <u>anything</u> while we listened to the breaking glass.
8. Mrs. White <u>strolled</u> out of the house.
9. Everybody <u>said</u>, "It was Ellen's idea!"
10. Mrs. White didn't care what <u>anybody</u> said, though.
11. b
12. c
13. a
14. Story should be edited for grammatical errors in subject-verb agreement, verb tense, and double negatives.

Home Alone
• Page 28
Answers will vary. Examples:
1. roll
2. concerned or worried
3. handle
4. scared
5. message
6. knock
7. laughed

Terrific Titles
• Page 29
1. c
2. b
3. c
4. a
5. c
6. a
7.–8. Answers will vary.

Big Facts
• Page 30
1. The largest ice cream sundae weighed over 10,000 pounds<u>.</u>
2. <u>H</u>igh school students and the <u>F</u>riendly <u>I</u>ce <u>C</u>ream <u>C</u>ompany made it in 1980<u>.</u>
3. <u>T</u>he biggest snowfall <u>was</u> in <u>C</u>olorado in April 1921<u>.</u>
4. <u>I</u>t snowed 76 inches in 24 <u>h</u>ours.
5. <u>T</u>he largest diamond <u>was</u> found in a mine in <u>S</u>outh <u>A</u>frica.
6. <u>I</u>t weigh<u>ed</u> over one and a half pounds<u>.</u>
7. Wilma <u>W</u>illiams <u>went</u> to 265 different schools when she was a child<u>.</u>

8. Author William <u>F</u>aulkner <u>wrote</u> one of the longest sentences in the world<u>.</u>
9. There <u>were</u> more than 1300 word<u>s</u> in it<u>!</u>
10. <u>A</u>mericans love pizza, and they eat 75 acres of pizza every day.
11. Americans eat 5,000 tons of candy a <u>day</u>.
12. Americans drink 17 million gallons of coffee and 6 million gallons of tea a day<u>.</u>

Mary's Letter
• Page 31
1. The letter should be edited for capitalization errors, punctuation, double negatives, spelling errors, subject-verb agreement. There are missing capitals in the address and opening, and missing capitals and punctuation in the closing.
2. Answers will vary.

Faraway Places
• Page 32
1. S
2. F
3. S
4. S
5. F
6. S
7.–8. Answers will vary. Examples: It is a very old city. Because running with the bulls can be dangerous, people are sometimes hurt.

Ghost Towns
• Page 33
1. simple
2. compound
3. simple
4. compound
5. simple
6. compound
7. a. and c. A few men found gold, and other men came to find gold.
8. b and c. Gold is what brought the men to the towns, but the gold soon ran out.

Pinknose
• Page 34
1. C
2. CX
3. C
4. S
5. CX
6. S
7. C
8. CX
9. C
10. S
11. C
12. C

The Train Ride
• Page 35
Answers may vary.
1. "All aboard!" the conductor yelled. He wore a blue suit.

2. Jessie stepped on board. It was her first train ride.
3. She was nervous. She sat near a window.
4. Jessie felt the train move, and she gasped out loud.
5. Soon, she saw farms and forests race by, and she gazed at the countryside.
6. Jessie held her carpetbag with both hands, and she put her hat on the seat.

Rodeos
• Page 36
  1. d
  2. b
  3. Answers will vary.
  4. the place where the first rodeo was held; how many towns today have rodeos

In the Details
• Page 37
  1. c
  2. b
  3. h
  4. g
  5. f
  6. d
  7. a
  8. e

Tornado!
• Page 38
  1. a, c, f
  2. c, d, f
  3. a, d, f

A Famous Flight
• Page 39
  1. b
  2. c
  3. b
  4. a.
  5. b
  6. Answers will vary. Example: what Lindbergh achieved for transportation later in his life.

Revolution
• Page 40
Sentences that should be crossed out:
1. Martha Custis had two children.
2. Martha came to the camp to see her husband. They were happy to see each other.
3. He also liked dogs. He had one dog named Sweet Lips.
4. Answers will vary.

The Windy City
• Page 41
  1. a; People in cities chose school boards, too.
  2. b; Fires are problems all over the world.
  3. c, d

Dreams
• Page 42
  1. b
  2. c
  3. a

Margo on Stage
• Page 43
  1. 5, 4, 9, 1, 12, 6, 2, 10, 11, 7, 13, 3, 8
Sentences that should be underlined: Margo chose to try out for the school play. She had play practice every night after school. The night of the play finally came.
  2. Answers will vary.

Balloon Rocket
• Page 44
Order of paragraphs: 3, 5, 2, 1, 4

The Contest
• Page 45
Story should be edited for spelling and punctuation. The first sentence should be indented, and other paragraph breaks occur at "The wind went first" and "Then it was the sun's turn."

Focus on Paragraphs
• Pages 46–47
  1. c
  2. b
  3. a
  4. d
  5. c
  6. c
  7. b
  8. c

Match Them Up
• Page 48
  1. b
  2. c
  3. b
  4. a
  5.–6. Answers will vary.

The Right Topics
• Page 49
  1. c
  2. b
  3. b
  4. d
  5. a
  6. c

The Right Fit
• Page 50
  1. b
  2. e
  3. c
  4. d
  5. a
  6. f

Author Tour
• Page 51
  1. Students should edit for spelling, capitalization in names and places, and punctuation. Unnecessary sentences are "I also really like Paula Danzinger's books." and "We stopped at Aunt

Answer Key

Mary's house." Paragraph breaks should be marked at the first sentence, at "First, we went to Lake Pepin"; "Then we drove to De Smet, South Dakota." and "Our last stop was in Missouri."
2. Audience: teachers and classmates
   Purpose: report on a summer vacation trip
3. Answers will vary.

Choose Your Words
• Pages 52–53
1. c
2. a
3. c
4. c
5. a
6. a
7. Crossed out: invisible. Possible replacement: cute
8. Crossed out: freezing. Possible replacement: green
9. Crossed out: high-tech. Possible replacement: curious
10. Crossed out: grew. Possible replacement: made
11. Crossed out: habitat. Possible replacement: cabin
12. Crossed out: cute. Possible replacement: division
13. Answers will vary.
14. Students should delete noisy, algebra, rock, and second. Replacement words will vary.

Careful Choices
• Page 54
1. c
2. a
3. b
4. c
5. Answers will vary.

Words About Lincoln
• Page 55
Students should take out *few, selections, town, move, carried, past,* and *interesting.* Replacement words will vary.
1. a
2. b
3. c

Check Your Sources
• Page 56
1. b
2. c
3. a
4. a
5. b
6. Answers will vary. Examples: encyclopedia, history atlas, books about specific tribes, Web sites
7. Answers will vary. Examples: a book about Japanese culture, a Web site with common Japanese words, an article about modern life in Tokyo

Spiders!
• Page 57
Underlined phrases: *two claws* (should be *per leg*); *do not run very fast* (should be *run very fast*); *lives underground* (should be *lives on a raft*); *a nest* (should be *a raft*)

Runaway Elephant
• Pages 58–59
1. 2 P.M.
2. Wrinkles
3. The zoo worker called the elephant that and was closer to Jan Walters so Jan probably heard it correctly.
4. The zoo worker had scattered them to attract the elephant.
5. in the woods
6. It broke down the door.
7.–10. Rewritten sentences will vary. Students should underline An African elephant named Wiggles . . . (should be *Wrinkles*); Friday morning (should be *afternoon*); They saw that the door to her pen had been left open. (should be *broken*); Old tracks . . . (should be *fresh tracks*); . . . showing that the elephant had been missing for a long time. (should be *a short time*); One visitor, Armand Leep . . . (should be *Lee*); . . . said he watched a zoo worker run into the woods. (It was Jan Walters who saw this happen.)

Fishing with Nick
• Pages 60–61
1. *Fly-Fishing for Beginners* (should be underlined in handwritten form)
2. 200 pages
3. at the library
4. Richard Lyle
5.–8. Rewritten sentences will vary. Students should underline: Rick Lyle (should be *Richard*); Mr. Lyle has always loved it. (He said that at first he hated it); eastern Montana (should be *western*); Gallatin River (should be *Clark Fork River* or *Bitterroot River*)

The Iroquois
• Pages 62–63
1. b
2. b
3. c
4. c
5. b
6. Answers will vary, but should include facts from the source materials.

Check It Out!
• Pages 64–65
1. all
2. b, d
3. b
4. a, b, d, e
5. a, b, d
6. b, c, d
7. a, c
8. Students should focus on spelling, capitalization, and punctuation, especially quotation marks.

Have a Heart!
• Page 66
1. Students should focus on spelling, capitalization, and punctuation, especially in the date, opening, and closing.
2. b, c, d
3. c

Answer Key

Did I Really Win?
- Page 67
  Editing should focus on commas in date line, opening, and closing. There are spelling, punctuation, and capitalization errors throughout the letter.

Colorful Nome
- Page 68
  1. d
  2. Students should indent paragraphs at "I remember how beautiful the Texas . . ."; "The people are colorful . . ."; "There are some things I love about . . . ." Editing focuses on spelling (particularly homophone errors). There are also punctuation and capitalization mistakes.

Ice Lanterns
- Page 69
  1. Students should edit for spelling, capitalization, punctuation, the extra word, the missing step and information, and grammatical errors.
  2. Possible answer: The water might freeze solid with no hole for the candle.
  3. c

Batting a Thousand
- Pages 70–71
  1. c
  2. a
  3. c
  4. Editing focus should be on spelling, capitalization, and punctuation. There is one missing piece of information, a paragraph out of order, and some homophone errors.
  5. c
  6. seven

The Greatest Invention
- Pages 72–73
  1. Editing should focus on main ideas and the details in the paragraphs. There are more spelling errors than other types.
  2. song, melody, drums, lullabies, marches
  3. c
  4. from the context of the sentence and the report
  5. Answers will vary.
  6. a

Wolves!
- Pages 74–75
  1. c
  2. a
  3. Answers will vary
  4. Students should check facts and quotations against the source material. There are capitalization, spelling, and indenting errors.

Water, Water Everywhere
- Pages 76–77
  1. c
  2. c
  3. b
  4. d
  5. The more you drink, the happier your body will be. (Other answers are possible.)

6. Drinking fountains are fun!
7. Editing should focus on spelling, capitalization, punctuation, and indenting. Also ensure that facts match the source material.

A Historic Birthday Party
- Pages 78–79
  1. Possible answers include not wanting to celebrate because of a population drop due to the Great River Flood.
  2. They were stopping only to hunt for food and rest.
  3. Focus editing on checking source material, especially dates; spelling, capitalization, and punctuation. There are some subject-verb mistakes as well.

Treasure!
- Pages 80–81
  1. long ago off the coast of Africa
  2. Captain Gomez, his crew, pirates, and the king
  3. Captain Gomez's ship cannot sail back to his country with the information he has due to the lack of wind and the possibility of pirates.
  4. The wind picks up; Captain Gomez sees and outruns the pirates.
  5. The wind moves Captain Gomez's ship faster than the pirates' ships, and he reaches his own country.
  6. a new French trade route
  7. Editing should focus on verb tense mistakes and mistakes with adverbs. There are also spelling, punctuation, capitalization, and other grammar errors. The final paragraph is not indented.

Caught in a Cave!
- Pages 82–83
  1. There are eight paragraphs in the story. They start at the first sentence, Already on this trip...; Then they had snapped a rope... "Don't worry..."; "I'm not worried..."; "I'll know in a minute..."; JoAnn waited in the pitch black.; "There's a passage..."
  2. The editing focus should be on indenting correctly and finding/punctuating all of the quotations in the dialogue. There are also a number of spelling errors.
  3. c
  4. Answers will vary

The Uncertain Trail
- Pages 84–85
  1. Students should edit for spelling, punctuation, capitalization, grammar, and indenting, and check for the accuracy and correct form of dates.
  2. Answers will vary. Possible answers include (1) a journal is set up by dated entries and (2) the story is told from only one person's point of view.
  3. b
  4. c
  5. Answers will vary.

The Great Oak Gang Mystery
- Pages 86–87
  1. Editing should focus on indenting of dialogue, as well as spelling, punctuation, and capitalization. There are several homophone errors.
  2. a, d
  3. The gang's tree house ladder is missing.
  4. The gang thought through the events and found the ladder in the bags with the leaves.

Answer Key

The Last Word
• Page 88
  1. a
  2. All of the items in Checklist A are needed for a poem. The items in Checklist B are not all needed, such as topic sentence and supporting details.
  3. The editing focus should be on capitals to begin each line, missing end marks at the ends of lines, spelling, and punctuation.

The Space Race
• Page 89
  1. The editing focus should be on capitalization, spelling, and punctuation. There is one missing word.
  2. In a story, every new sentence needs to begin with a capital. In a poem, each line begins with a capital letter.

The River King
• Pages 90–91
  1. The editing focus should be on spelling, capitalization, extra words, and punctuation.
  2. c
  3. d
  4. d
  5. c

Back to Basics
• Pages 92–93
  1. On December 7, 1941, the Japanese attacked Pearl Harbor.
  2. Our old house was in Central City, Kansas.
  3. "Could we please," Carl asked his grandma, "have some ice cream?"
  4. Dr. Shard asked us to come by his office on Tuesday.
  5. d
  6. a
  7. d
  8. b
  9. After all of that, we still didn't know how Edward would get to John's game.
  10. "Do you want to go to the ball now?" asked Cinderella's fairy godmother.
  11. The letter needs the date corrected; capitalization in the date line, opening, both sentences, the closing, and the signature. There is also a missing apostrophe and missing commas.
  12. all
  13. b
  14. c

Spell Well
• Page 94
  1. c
  2. a
  3. d
  4. d
  5. d
  6. c
  7. b
  8. all

Can You *Sea* What I Mean?
• Page 95
  1. great

  2. scent
  3. read, whole, hour
  4. meet
  5. principal
  6. rowed
  7. shone
  8. Dear
  9. Whose
  10. through
  11. You're, to, right
  12. your, their
  13. You're, tied, steal, sees, team, there, peace, where, right, their, might, minor
  14. Examples: letters, stories, reports, explanations, notes, lists, poems, instructions, homework, answers, and essays

Farm Life
• Page 96
  1. c
  2. a
  3. b
  4. a
  5. have
  6. leaves, works
  7. are
  8. brushes
  9. By the Fourth of July, Dad knows whether the crops will turn out well.
  10. All last winter, we enjoyed Mother's canned tomatoes.
  11. The horses pull the wagons, but the oxen pull the plow.
  12. I love the farm.

Secret to Success
• Page 97
  1. Example: Markita and Travis ran to the motorcycle. When Markita started the motorcycle, Travis jumped on.
  2. Sentences will vary.
  3. Example: Travis hopped in the car and drove away. When he got to the cave, he parked the car inside and got out of the car.
  4. Under cover of night, the two spies fled the city.
  5. In preparing his report, Travis made sure he stated the facts correctly.

Anchor Your Ideas
• Page 98
  1. b
  2. c
  3. c
  4. d
  5. b, c, d, f

Get the Point?
• Page 99
  1. Begin paragraphs at "Do you… " and "Pedro answered… "
  2. Begin paragraphs at "Another mistake …" and "The last trick…"

The Key Word
• Page 100
  1. a
  2. a or c

3. c
4. a
5. b
6.–7. Answers will vary. Examples:
6. That scary street is just too busy for us to cross.
7. Please help make the street safe to cross by considering the installation of a traffic light.

Tell Me Why
• Page 101
  1. c
  2. a
  3. a
  4. a
  5. f
  6. e
  7. g
  8. d
  9. c
  10. b

Not-So-Dandy Handy-Dandy
• Page 102
  Checklist should include commas after greeting and closing, comma between date and year, spelling, punctuation, capitalization, grammar, indenting. Students should edit all of these items in the letter.

A Special Grandfather
• Page 103
  Checklist should include commas after greeting and closing, comma between date and year, spelling, punctuation, capitalization, grammar, indenting. Students should edit all of these items in the letter. There are no mistakes in the opening dialogue that sets up the letter.

The Man and the Cat
• Pages 104–105
  1. Checklist should include checking facts against the sources, topic sentences and supporting details, spelling, capitalization, punctuation, and grammar. There is one incorrect date in the report.
  2. 1939–1945—wrote training movies for the U.S. Army; 1984—won a Pulitzer Prize
  3. They were not important to his writing of children's books, which is the main idea of the report.
  4. c

Stonehenge
• Pages 106–107
  1. Two dates are incorrect in the report: 2000 B.C. should be 3000 B.C., and 1500 B.C. should be 1100 B.C.
  2. Checklist should include checking facts against the sources, topic sentences and supporting details, spelling, capitalization, punctuation, grammar, and indenting. Students should check the accuracy of the quotes from the author and find the incorrect dates.

Olaf's Adventure
• Pages 108–109
  1. b
  2. Olaf sees something move but doesn't know what it is. It may be dangerous.

3. b
4. Olaf sees the night worm and realizes that there is no danger.
5. Checklist should include punctuation, capitalization, spelling, indenting, beginning, middle, and end. Students should mark all paragraphs that are not indented. There are more spelling errors than other types.

A Bittersweet Day
• Pages 110–111
  1. Checklist should include punctuation, capitalization, spelling, indenting, beginning, middle, and end. Students should notice that one exchange between Alex and her mother appears on the same line and that the final paragraph is not indented.
  2. b
  3. happy and sad at the same time

Make It Even Better
• Page 112
  1–4: Answers will vary.

Make It Your Best!
• Page 113
  1–2: Answers will vary.

Cadillac Lake
• Page 114
  Revision should make the letter clearer. Students should rewrite the section of sentences that all run together and eliminate the unnecessary repetitions.

Homemade Ice Cream
• Page 115
  Clear and complete steps include adding the large bag to the supplies, noting the other necessary items in step 2, placing smaller bag inside larger bag, and moving step 3 after step 5.

Waste Not, Want Not
• Pages 116–117
  1. Trash is really gross and often smells bad.
  2. Answers will vary.
  3. Answers will vary, but should include plastic, glass, and one of the others.
  4. Answers will vary.
  5. Answers will vary. Example: Together we can help keep our planet healthy.

A Very Cold Journey
• Pages 118–119
  Revisions will vary.
  1. Revision should focus on combining and varying sentences, such as "Ice was everywhere. It surrounded our small ship from port to starboard. Ice was all we could see all the way to the horizon. It made creaking and groaning noises as it slowly crushed our ship."
  2. Revision should focus on a logical order of presenting the details in the paragraph. Some details are out of sequence, and there is some repetition.
  3. Revision should focus on shortening the paragraph.
  4. Example: "Our only hope was to rescue ourselves. We built small sleds from the ship's planks. After loading our gear, we walked across the ice, climbing over rocks and running over broken ice bridges . . . ." etc.

Proofreading Marks

Capitalize a letter: w̲.

bi̲lbo ba̲ggins

Lowercase a letter: Ø.

House

Delete a letter or a word: ℓ.

the ~~the~~ big ogre.

Change the order of letters or words: ∪ .

recieve

Add a word, a period, a comma or other punctuation: ⌄ ⌃ ⌃"

of
The Lord ⌃ the Rings

Show start of a new paragraph: ¶ .

That's why I really like astronomy. ¶Another favorite pasttime I have is studying dinosaurs. My collection of dinosaur resources includes several books, models, and a real fossil I found while visiting Arizona.

 0-7424-2754-4 *Proofreading & Editing*